CHURCHILL
IN "QUOTES"

WIT AND WISDOM FROM
THE GREAT STATESMAN

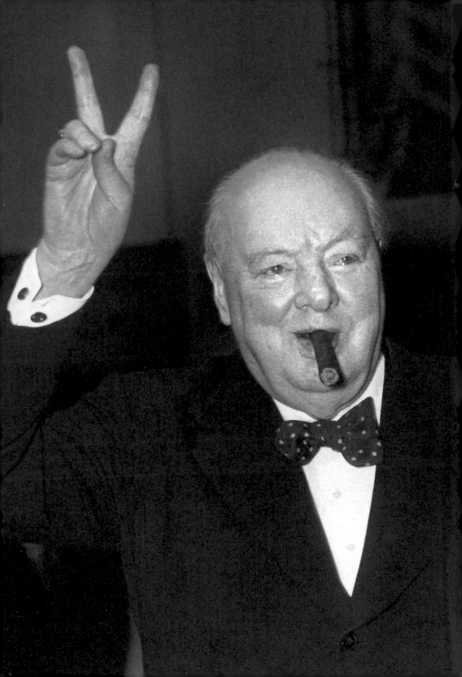

CHURCHILL

IN "QUOTES"

WIT AND WISDOM FROM
THE GREAT STATESMAN

AMMONITE
PRESS

pa media

"If you have knowledge, let others light their candles with it."

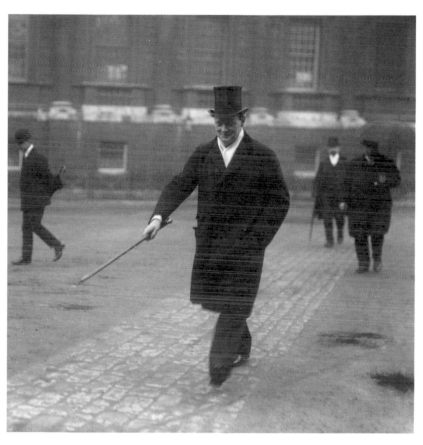

Home Secretary Winston Churchill leaves the House of Commons.
1911

INTRODUCTION

In the autobiography of his early life, *My Early Life: A Roving Commission*, published in 1930, Winston Churchill wrote, 'Twenty to twenty-five, those are the years.' Indeed, before he had reached the age of twenty-six, he had experienced combat in Cuba, India and Africa, been mentioned in despatches and awarded four medals, written several books, become a national hero and been elected as a member of Parliament. Many would settle for that as a lifetime's achievement, but for Churchill there was so much more to come, and even in 1930, at the age of fifty-six, his 'finest hour' was still some way in the future.

Born in 1874, the son of a prominent Tory politician and member of the aristocracy, Lord Randolph Churchill, and American socialite Jennie Jerome, Winston Leonard Spencer Churchill was destined to become one of the outstanding figures of the twentieth century. He is considered by many to be the greatest Briton of all time.

Twice Prime Minister and the holder at one time or another of all the important cabinet posts in government, this great statesman would lead the nation through the dark days of the Second World War, a beacon of defiance in the face of German, Italian and Japanese aggression that threatened to consume much of the world. His powerful oratory was an inspiration to the British people, giving them hope when their backs were to the wall.

Indeed, Churchill was a master of rhetoric: his speeches, radio broadcasts and writings bristled and sparkled with uplifting phrases, cutting remarks and wry wit, while his off-the-cuff comments were legendary. In 1953, he was awarded the Nobel Prize in Literature for 'his mastery of historical and biographical description as well as for brilliant oratory in defending exalted human values'.

Here then, for the purposes of criticism and review, is a sample of Winston Churchill's adroitness with the English language, a celebration of his way with words that will amuse and inspire. For practically all of the great man's public life, the skilled photographers of the Press Association were on hand to record the events in which he participated. Their work provides a fascinating visual accompaniment to the text.

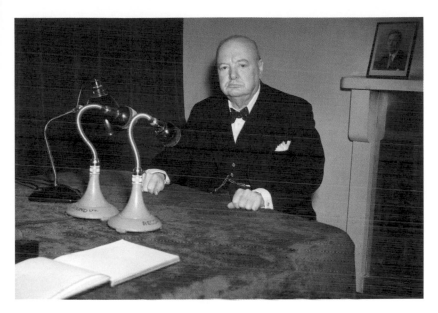

Winston Churchill, in preparation for the coming General Election,
records an election speech at a studio in London.
28 September, 1951

"The object of Parliament is to substitute argument for fisticuffs."

Speech, House of Commons, 6 June 1951.

"I remember, when I was a child, being taken to the celebrated Barnum's circus, which contained an exhibition of freaks and monstrosities. But the exhibit ... which I most desired to see was ... 'The Boneless Wonder'. My parents judged that that spectacle would be too revolting and demoralizing for my youthful eyes, and I have waited fifty years to see the boneless wonder sitting on the Treasury Bench."

On Prime Minister Ramsay MacDonald, speech, House of Commons, 28 January 1931.

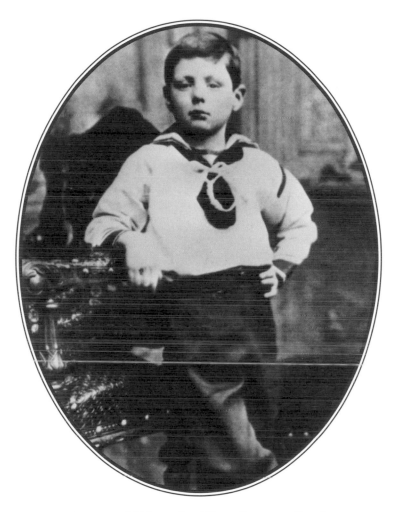

Seven-year-old Winston Churchill proudly wears a sailor suit.
1881

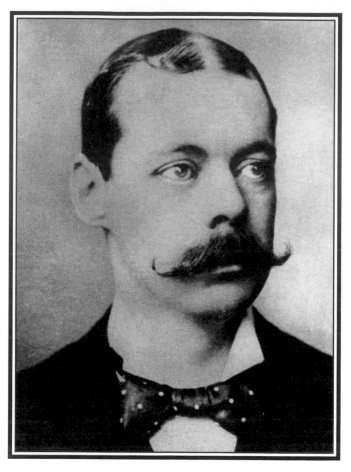

Lord Randolph Churchill, father of Winston.
1885

"Saving is a fine thing. Especially when your parents have done it for you."

"Although always prepared for martyrdom, I preferred that it should be postponed."

On military training at Sandhurst, *My Early Life: A Roving Commission,* 1930.

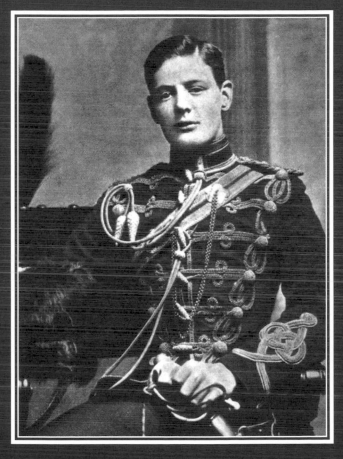

Winston Churchill as a cornet (second lieutenant)
in the 4th Queen's Own Hussars.
1895

"Nothing in life is so exhilarating as to be shot at without result."

The Story of the Malakand Field Force:
An Episode of Frontier War, 1898.

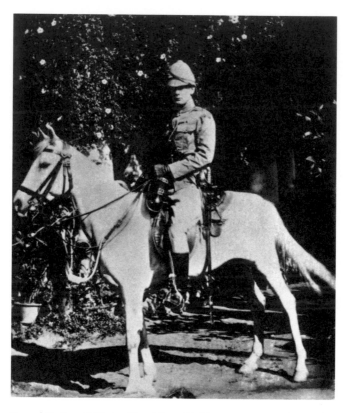

Second Lieutenant Winston Churchill outside his quarters in Bangalore, India.
1897

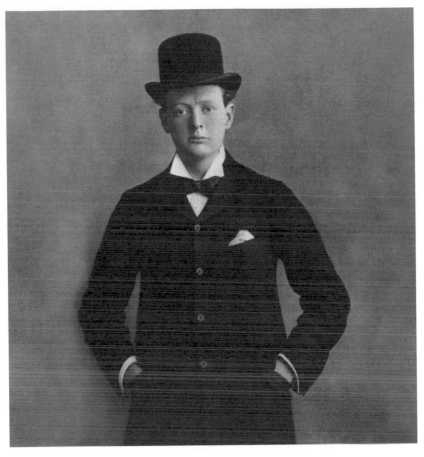

Conservative candidate for Oldham, the first seat to be fought by
the future prime minister.
1899

"Success is the ability to go from one failure
to another with no loss of enthusiasm."

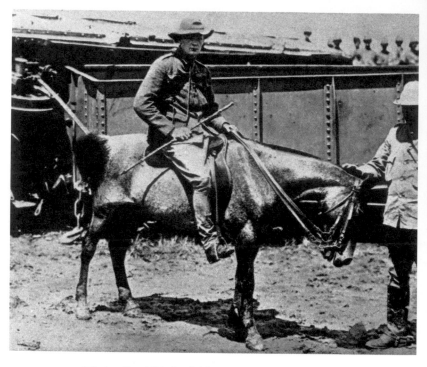

Winston Churchill in South Africa as a war correspondent for
The Morning Post during the Second Boer War.
1899

"Keep cool, men.
This will be interesting
for my paper."

When rallying the occupants of an armoured reconnaissance train ambushed
during the Second Anglo-Boer War in South Africa by Boer forces,
November 1900.

"This is no time for ease and comfort. It is time to dare and endure."

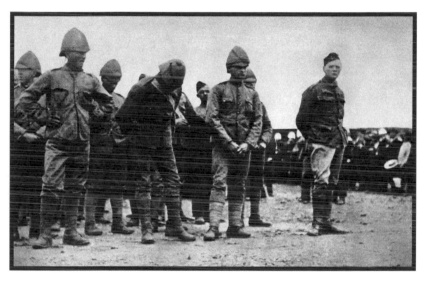

Winston Churchill (R) as a prisoner of war in Pretoria, South Africa.
1899

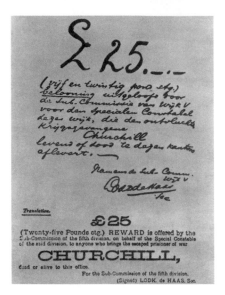

A wanted notice for Winston Churchill, issued after he escaped from a prisoner-of-war camp in South Africa.
1899

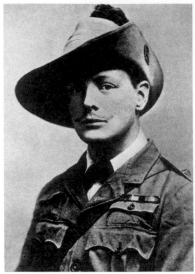

Winston Churchill in the uniform of the South African Light Horse cavalry unit during the Second Boer War.
1899

"Never, never, never believe any war will be smooth and easy, or that anyone who embarks on the strange voyage can measure the tides and hurricanes he will encounter. ... Always remember, however sure you are that you could easily win, that there would not be a war if the other man did not think he also had a chance."

On war in South Africa, *My Early Life: A Roving Commission*, 1930.

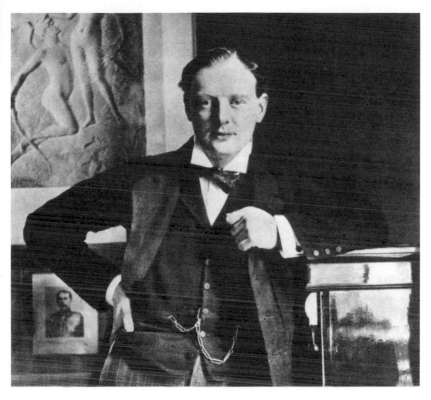

Winston Churchill when he first took his seat in the House of Commons.
1 February 1901

"The ability to foretell what is going to
happen tomorrow, next week, next month,
and next year — and to have the ability
afterwards to explain why it didn't happen."

On the qualities required by a politician, newspaper interview, 1902.

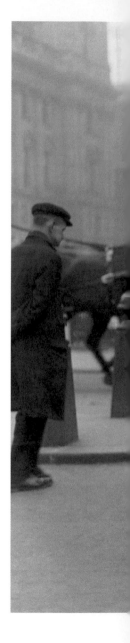

"For my own part, I have always felt that a politician is to be judged by the animosities which he excites among his opponents. I have always set myself not merely to relish, but to deserve thoroughly their censure."

Speech, Institute of Journalists dinner, London, 17 November 1906.

Under-Secretary of State for the Colonies Winston Churchill on his way to the Houses of Parliament. 1 September 1905

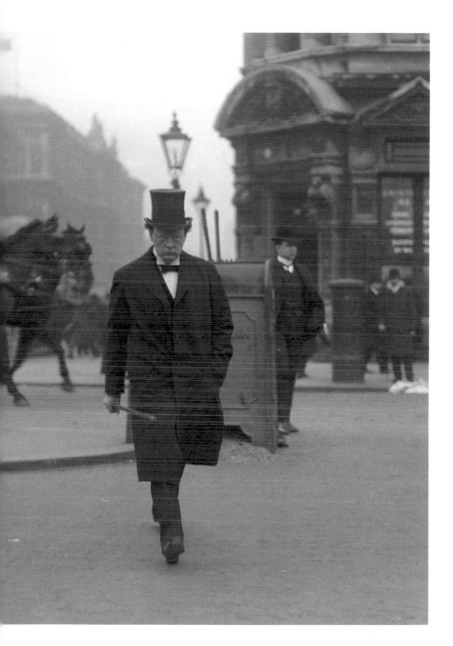

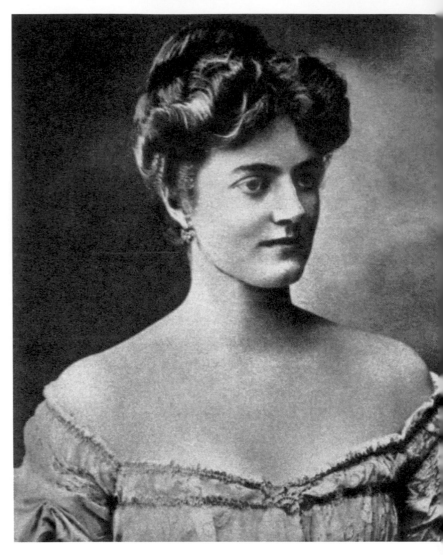

Winston Churchill with Clementine Hozier in the year of their engagement.
1908

CHURCHILL IN QUOTES

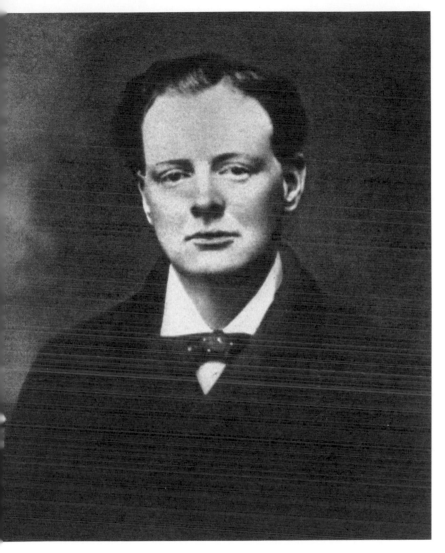

"My most brilliant achievement was to persuade my wife to marry me."

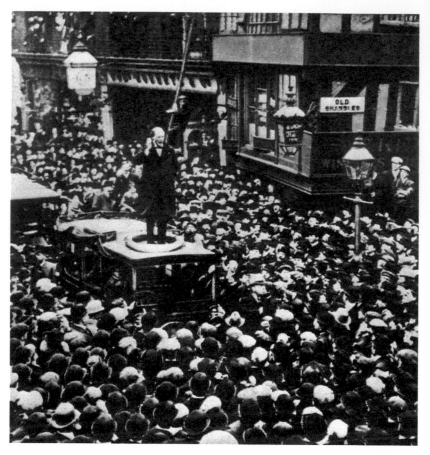

Winston Churchill, as a Liberal, addressing a crowd in the 1908 by-election in Manchester North West, caused by his appointment as President of the Board of Trade.
1 June 1908

"Healthy citizens are the greatest asset any country can have."

"India is a geographical term. It is no more a united nation than the equator."

Speech, Royal Albert Hall, London, 18 March 1931.

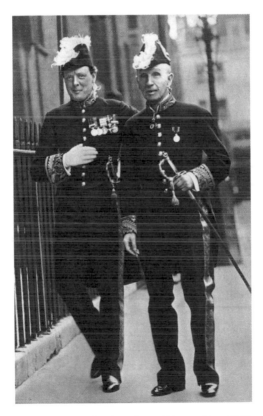

Under-Secretary of State for the Colonies Winston Churchill (L) arrives at 10 Downing Street with John Morley, Secretary of State for India. 7 July 1908

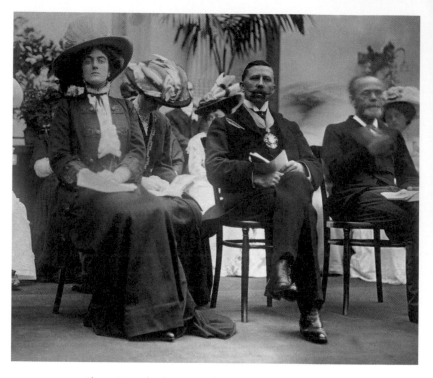

Clementine, wife of Winston Churchill, and Lord Cheylesmore,
Mayor of Westminster, at a bazaar in aid of the Browning Settlement.
1909

"My wife and I tried two or three times in the
last few years to have breakfast together,
but it was so disagreeable we had to stop."

"At every crisis the Kaiser crumpled.
In defeat he fled; in revolution he abdicated;
in exile he remarried."

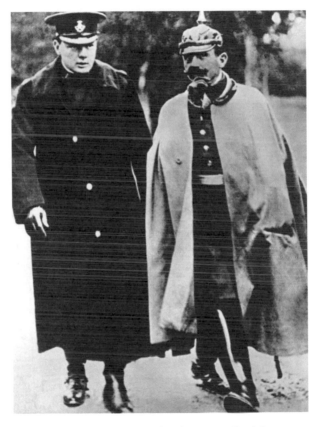

President of the Board of Trade Winston Churchill
and German Kaiser Wilhelm II.
2 October 1909

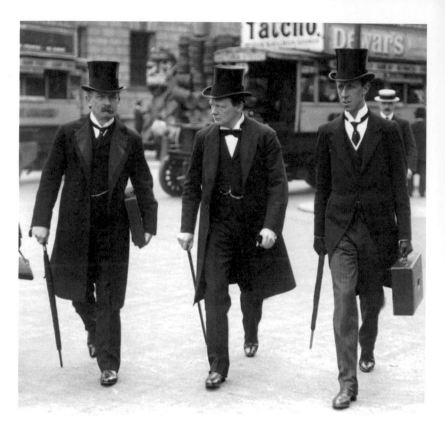

L–R: Chancellor of the Exchequer David Lloyd George with Winston Churchill and Mr Clarke. 1910

"Attitude is a little thing that makes a big difference."

"What is the use of living, if it be not to strive for noble causes and to make this muddled world a better place for those who will live in it after we are gone?

... Humanity will not be cast down. We are going on swinging bravely forward along the grand high road and already behind the distant mountains is the promise of the sun."

Speech on unemployment, Dundee, 10 October 1908.

"Battles are won by slaughter and manoeuvre. The greater the general, the more he contributes in manoeuvre, the less he demands in slaughter."

The World Crisis, Vol 2, 1923.

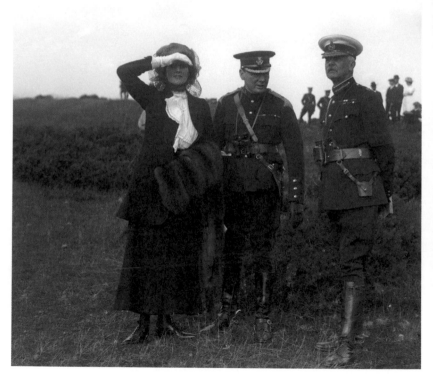

Home Secretary Winston Churchill (C) with his wife Clementine and General Bruce Hamilton watching Army manoeuvres at Aldershot.
1 June 1910

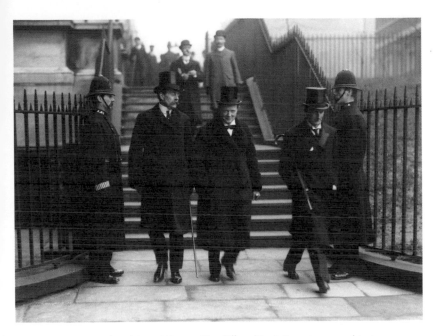

L–R: Sir Edward Grey, Winston Churchill and Lord Crewe leave a cabinet meeting following the Liberal victory in the General Election.
14 February 1910

"If you have an important point to make, don't try to be subtle or clever. Use a pile driver. Hit the point once. Then come back and hit it again. Then hit it a third time – a tremendous whack."

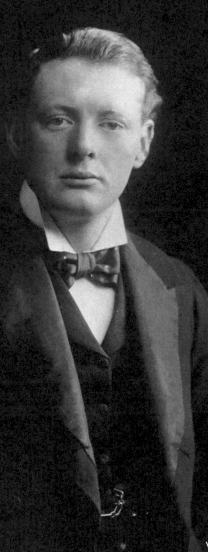

"Of course I am an egoist. Where do you get if you aren't?"

Winston Churchill as Home Secretary.
1 November 1910

"I have taken more out of alcohol than alcohol has taken out of me."

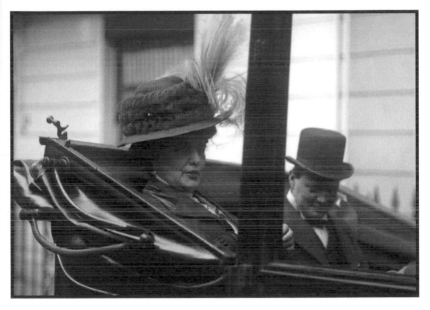

Winston Churchill with his mother, Mrs Cornwallis-West (Lady Randolph Churchill).
1911

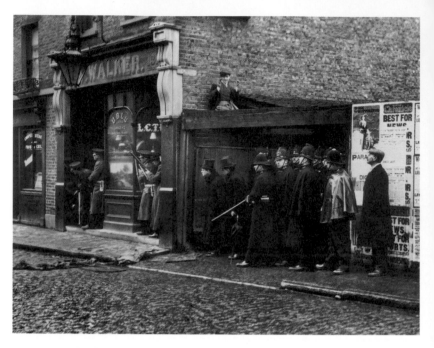

Winston Churchill (C, top hat) during the siege of Sidney Street in Stepney, East London.
3 January 1911

"I never worry about action, but only about inaction."

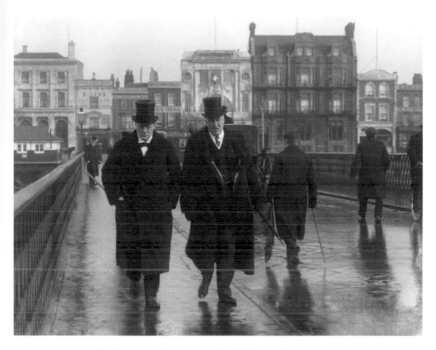

First Lord of the Admiralty Winston Churchill (L) and his private secretary,
Rear Admiral Sir Ernest Charles Thomas Troubridge.
4 April 1911

"The honourable gentleman should not really generate more indignation than he can conveniently contain."

To an MP who kept standing and interrupting him.

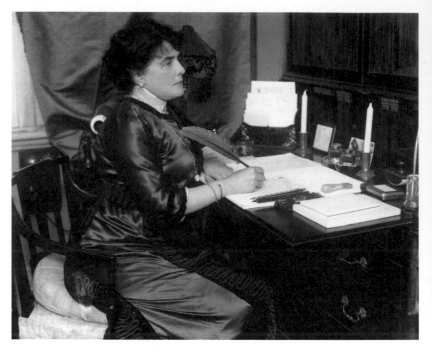

Winston Churchill's mother, Mrs Cornwallis-West, at home. After the death of his father,
she had married George Cornwallis-West, but later divorced him.
1912

"She shone for me like the Evening Star. I loved her dearly — but at a distance."

On his mother, Lady Randolph Churchill,
My Early Life: A Roving Commission, 1930.

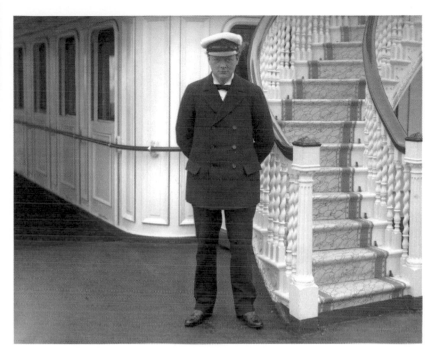

First Lord of the Admiralty Winston Churchill aboard the Royal yacht at Cowes.
1912

"Courage is what it takes to stand up and speak; courage is also what it takes to sit down and listen."

"Everything tends towards catastrophe and collapse. I am interested, geared up and happy. Is it not horrible to be made like this?"

In a letter to his wife Clementine during the build-up to the First World War.

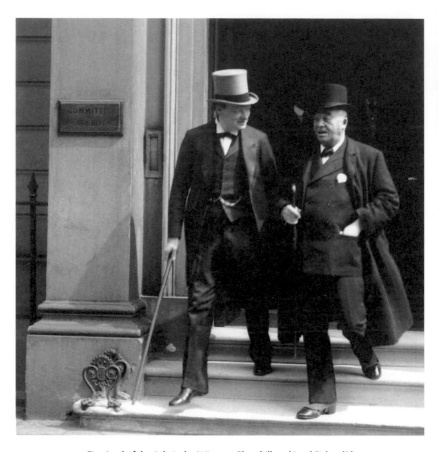

First Lord of the Admiralty Winston Churchill and Lord Fisher (R)
leave a meeting of the Imperial Defence Committee.
1913

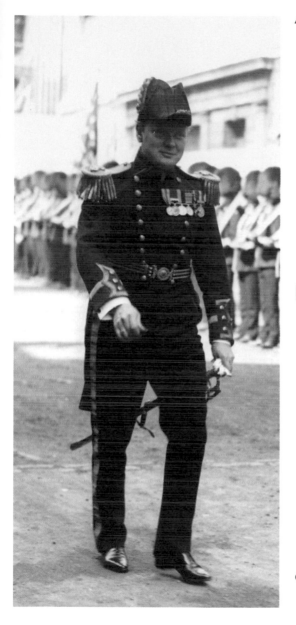

"Too often the strong, silent man is silent only because he does not know what to say, and is reputed strong only because he has remained silent."

Winston S. Churchill: His Complete Speeches, Volume IV: 1922–1928, 1974.

Winston Churchill, in the uniform of the Elder Brother of Trinity House, leaves the Guildhall, London, during the visit of the French President. 1913

"In war it does not matter who is right, but who is left."

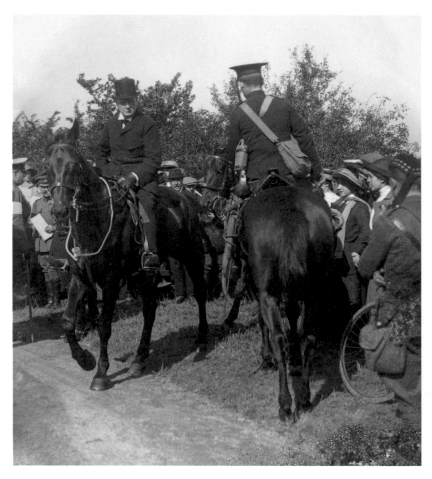

First Lord of the Admiralty Winston Churchill attending
Army manoeuvres at Towcester, Northamptonshire.
7 June 1913

CHURCHILL IN QUOTES

"We are masters of the unsaid words, but slaves of those we let slip out."

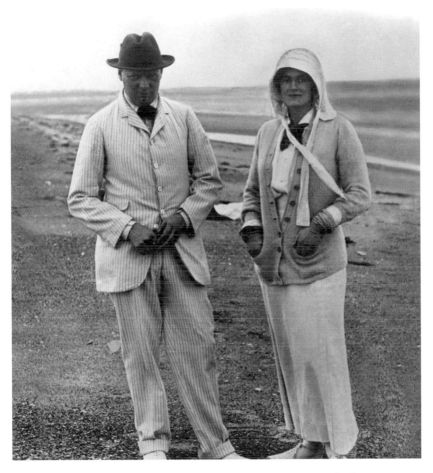

Winston Churchill and his wife Clementine during a holiday at Sandwich, Kent.
1 March 1914

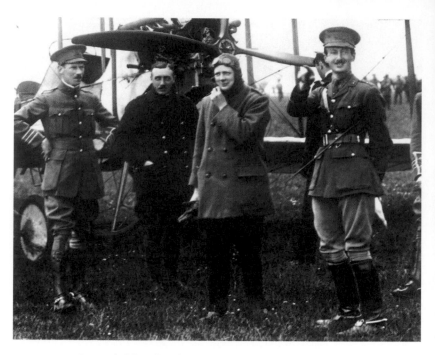

First Lord of the Admiralty Winston Churchill arrives at Portsmouth
in an Army biplane, piloted by Major Gerrard.
29 April 1914

"I am a sporting man. I always give them a fair chance to get away."

In answer to why he missed so many trains and aeroplanes.

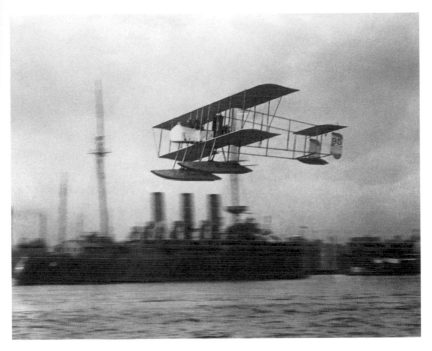

A seaplane carries First Lord of the Admiralty Winston Churchill over Portsmouth Harbour.
5 May 1914

"If the Almighty were to rebuild the world and asked me for advice, I would have English Channels round every country. And the atmosphere would be such that anything which attempted to fly would be set on fire."

"[The] truth is incontrovertible. Panic may resent it, ignorance may deride it, malice may distort it, but there it is."

Speech, House of Commons, 17 May 1916.

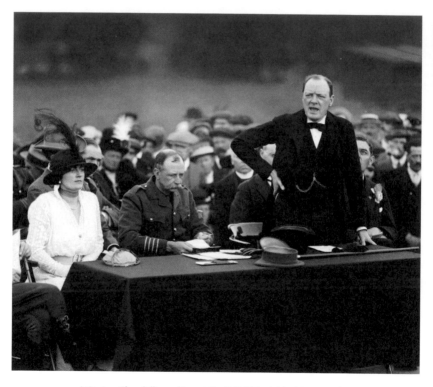

Winston Churchill speaking at the Enfield Lock Munitions Works.
His wife Clementine is seated on the left.
1915

"Politics are very much like war.
We may even have to use
poison gas at times."

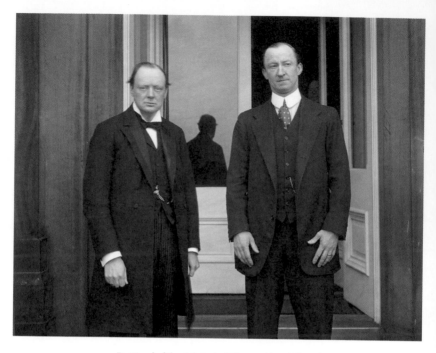

First Lord of the Admiralty Winston Churchill and
Parliamentary Secretary to the Treasury Percy Illingworth.
5 May 1915

"I think a curse should rest on me — because
I love this war. I know it's smashing and
shattering the lives of thousands every
moment — and yet — I can't help it
— I enjoy every second of it."

In a letter to a friend, 1916.

"A prisoner of war is a man who tries to kill you and fails, and then asks you not to kill him."

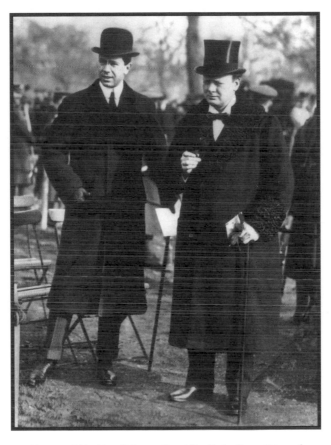

Minister of Munitions Winston Churchill with the Crown Prince of Sweden, Gustaf VI Adolf, at a review of the Army of Occupation in Hyde Park, London.
1917

"The United States invariably does the right thing, after having exhausted every other alternative."

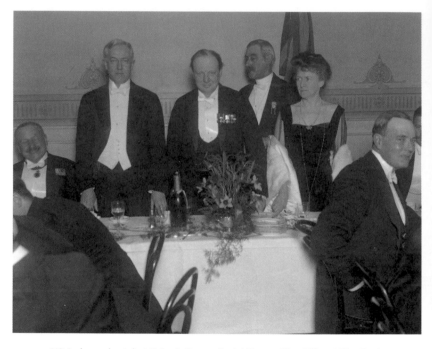

US Ambassador John W. Davis (L, standing), Winston Churchill and Ellen Davis at an English Speaking Union dinner in honour of the ambassador.
1919

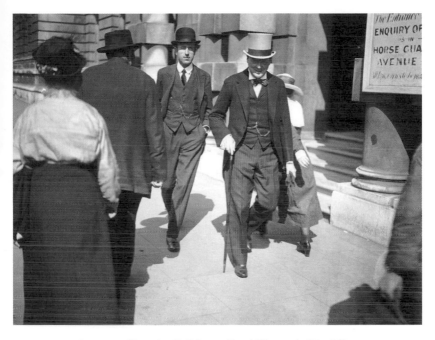

Secretary of State for Air Winston Churchill leaves the War Office
with newly appointed Air Council member Lord Londonderry.
1919

"We have always found the Irish a bit odd.
They refuse to be English."

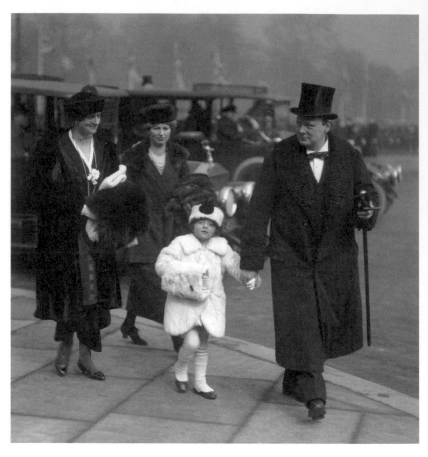

Winston Churchill, his wife Clementine and their daughter Sarah arrive to watch
the Brigade of Guards in a march past in The Mall.
22 January 1919

"Great and good are
seldom the same man."

"It is a fine thing to be honest, but it is also very important to be right."

"The object of presenting medals, stars and ribbons is to give pride and pleasure to those who have deserved them. At the same time, a distinction is something which everybody does not possess.
If all have it, it is of less value ...
A medal glitters, but it also casts a shadow."

Speech on war decorations, House of Commons, 22 March 1944.

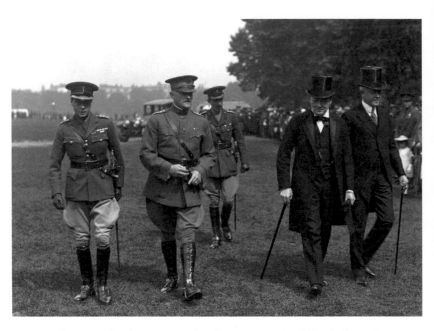

L–R: The Prince of Wales, US General Pershing, Winston Churchill and John W. Davis, US Ambassador, arrive at Hyde Park, London for an investiture.
19 July 1919

"Lenin was sent into Russia by the Germans in the same way that you might send a phial containing a culture of typhoid or cholera to be poured into the water supply of a great city, and it worked with amazing accuracy."

Speech on Vladimir Lenin, House of Commons, 5 November 1919.

"History is written by the victors."

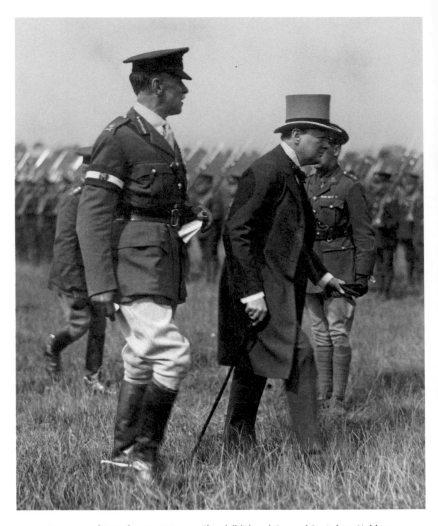

Secretary of State for War Winston Churchill (R) and General Sir Aylmer Haldane review British occupation forces in Cologne, Germany.
5 August 1920

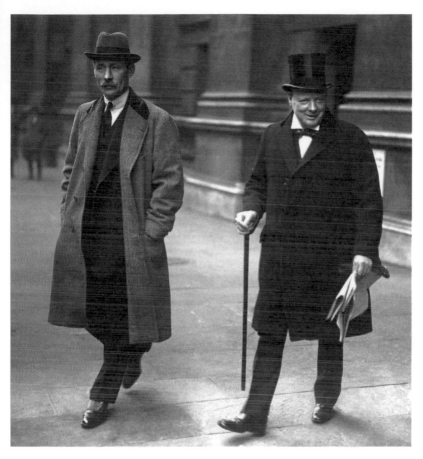

Winston Churchill (R) leaves the Colonial Office with Captain Sir Frederick Guest.
11 April 1921

"Some people regard private enterprise
as a predatory tiger to be shot. Others look on
it as a cow they can milk. Not enough people see it
as a healthy horse, pulling a sturdy wagon."

"You will make all kinds of mistakes; but as long as you are generous and true, and also fierce, you cannot hurt the world or even seriously distress her."

On military training at Sandhurst, *My Early Life: A Roving Commission*, 1930.

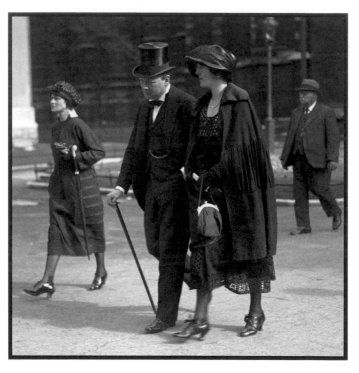

Winston Churchill and his wife Clementine arrive at Westminster Abbey for a memorial service for Admiral of the Fleet Sir Arthur Knyvet Wilson.
31 May 1921

"There are a terrible lot of lies going around the world, and the worst of it is half of them are true."

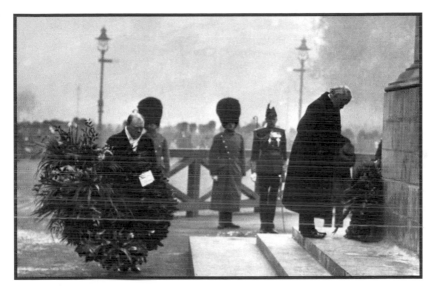

Prime Minister David Lloyd George (R) and Secretary of State for War Winston Churchill lay wreaths at the Cenotaph, London, on Armistice Day. 11 November 1921

"Never hold discussions with the monkey when the organ grinder is in the room."

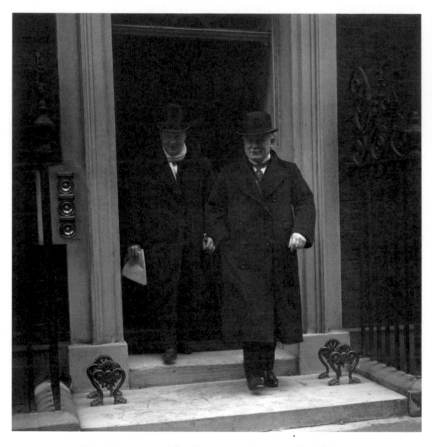

Prime Minister David Lloyd George and Winston Churchill leave
10 Downing Street for the House of Commons.
10 February 1922

"I always manage somehow to adjust to any new level of luxury without whimper or complaint. It is one of my more winning traits."

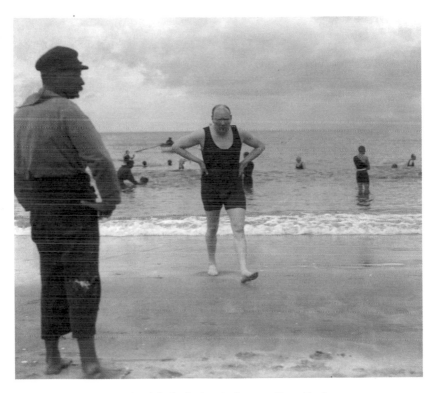

Winston Churchill after bathing in the sea at Deauville, France.
1 August 1922

"No hour of life is lost that is spent in the saddle."

My Early Life: A Roving Commission, 1930.

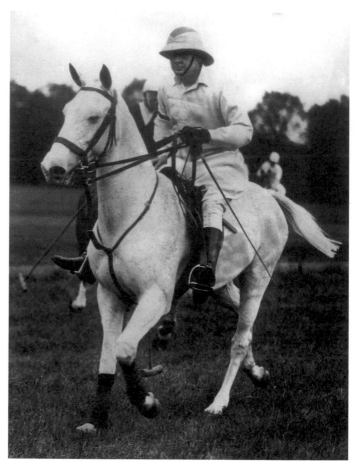

Winston Churchill playing polo at Worcester Park, London.
1923

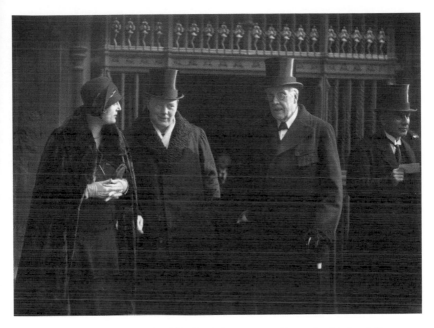

Clementine and Winston Churchill (C) with former Prime Minister Lord Arthur Balfour.
12 November 1923

"If you wanted nothing done at all, Balfour was the man for the job."

On Lord Arthur Balfour.

"I do think unpunctuality is a vile habit, and all my life I have tried to break myself of it."

My Early Life: A Roving Commission, 1930.

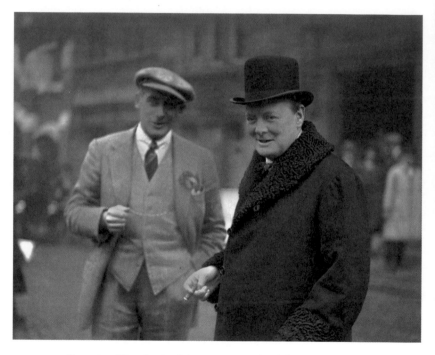

Secretary of State for the Colonies Winston Churchill with his secretary,
Lord John 'Jack' Wodehouse, a noted polo player.
21 November 1923

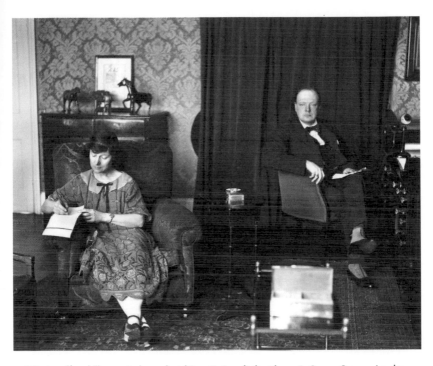

Winston Churchill as an Independent (Constitutionalist), at home in Sussex Square, London, with his secretary prior to the Westminster Abbey by-election.
6 March 1924

"A sheep in sheep's clothing."

On Labour leader Ramsay MacDonald.

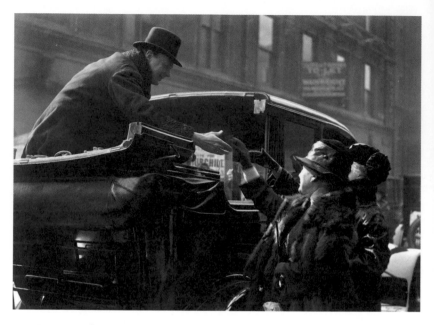

Constitutionalist Winston Churchill is greeted by a supporter while campaigning for the Westminster Abbey by-election, which was won by the Conservatives.
19 March 1924

"The biggest argument against democracy is a five-minute discussion with the average voter."

"Socialism is the philosophy of failure, the creed of ignorance and the gospel of envy."

Winston Churchill (R), stands in a car while being chased by jeering socialists after the Westminster Abbey by-election.
21 March 1924

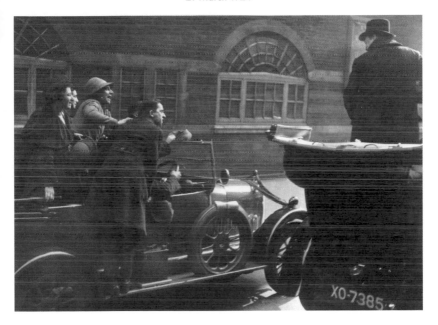

"I do not resent criticism, even when, for the sake of emphasis, it parts for the time with reality."

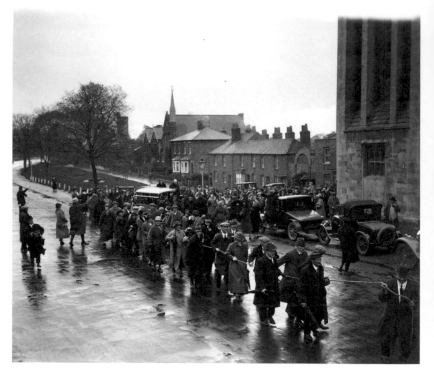

Winston Churchill and his wife Clementine are hauled through the streets after he was returned as the Constitutionalist MP for Epping in the 1924 General Election.
30 October 1924

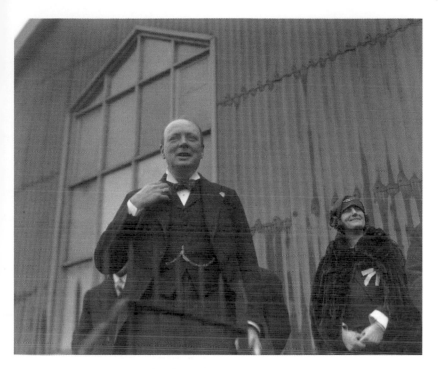

Winston Churchill addresses the crowd on election day at Epping.
30 October 1924

"Anyone can rat; it takes a certain amount of ingenuity to re-rat."

On switching from the Conservative Party to the Liberals and then back to the Conservatives, 1924.

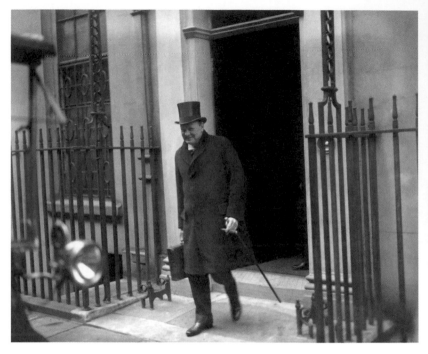

Chancellor of the Exchequer Winston Churchill leaves 10 Downing Street.
27 April 1925

"Occasionally he stumbled over the truth, but hastily picked himself up and hurried on as if nothing had happened."

On Conservative Prime Minister Stanley Baldwin.

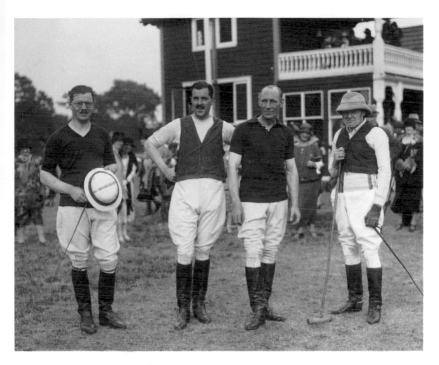

Winston Churchill (R) and other members of the House of Commons
polo team during their match against the Lords.
1 June 1925

"I am certainly not one of those who need to be prodded. In fact, if anything, I am the prod."

"One ought never to turn one's back on a threatened danger and try to run away from it. If you do that, you will double the danger. But if you meet it promptly and without flinching, you will reduce the danger by half."

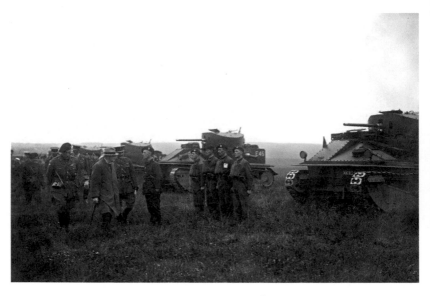

Chancellor of the Exchequer Winston Churchill inspects a troop from the Royal Tank Corps. 1927

CHURCHILL IN QUOTES

"Do stop interrupting me
while I am interrupting you!"

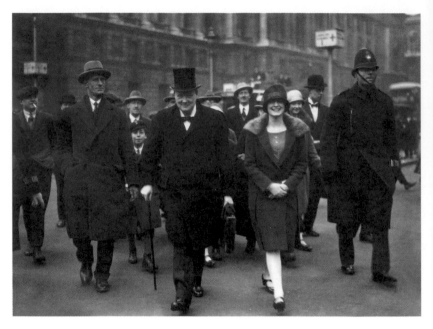

Chancellor of the Exchequer Winston Churchill arrives with his daughter Diana to deliver the annual Budget at the House of Commons.
11 April 1927

"Everyone threw the blame on me. I have noticed that they nearly always do. I suppose it is because they think I shall be able to bear it best."

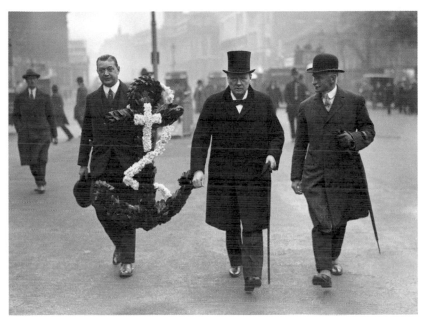

Winston Churchill arrives with the RND wreath on Anzac Day at Whitehall.
25 April 1927

"The longer you can look back, the farther
you can look forward."

"I neither want it [brandy] nor need it, but I should think it pretty hazardous to interfere with the ineradicable habit of a lifetime."

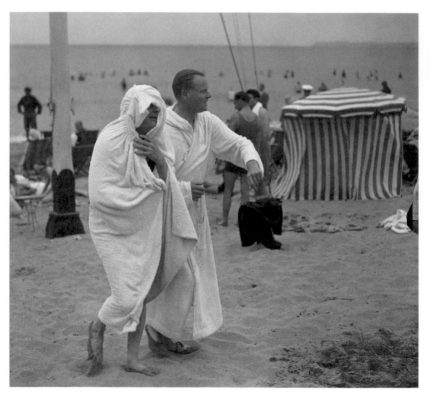

Chancellor of the Exchequer Winston Churchill (L) and the Duke of Sutherland wrap themselves in robes after taking a dip in the sea.
1 August 1927

"War is a game that is played with a smile. If you can't smile, grin. If you can't grin, keep out of the way till you can."

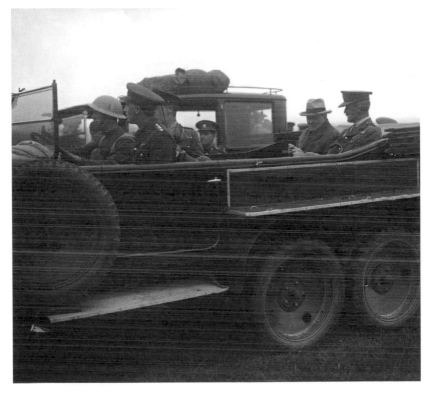

Chancellor of the Exchequer Winston Churchill rides in a troop carrier while inspecting mechanized forces at Tidworth, Hampshire.
31 August 1927

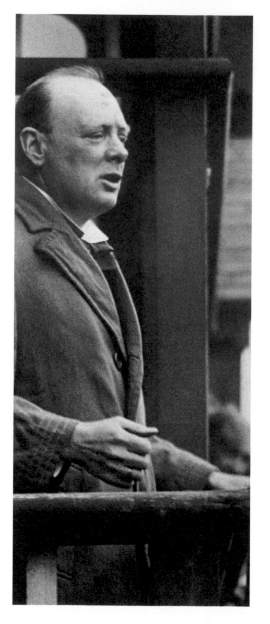

"So little time, so much to do."

In response to a woman who challenged him on his alcohol consumption during an election speech in a church hall. The woman claimed that during his lifetime he had consumed enough alcohol to fill the hall to a point halfway up the walls. Churchill looked at her and at the point she was indicating on the wall, then allowed his gaze to travel to the ceiling before uttering the words.

Winston Churchill addresses an election meeting at Epping in Essex. 1929

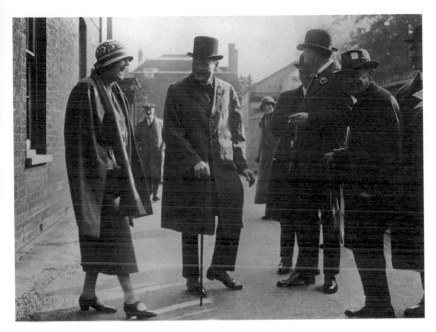

Winston Churchill (C) and his wife Clementine in Epping, Essex,
for an election meeting.
1929

"I wish Stanley Baldwin no ill, but it would have been much better if he had never lived."

On Conservative leader Stanley Baldwin.

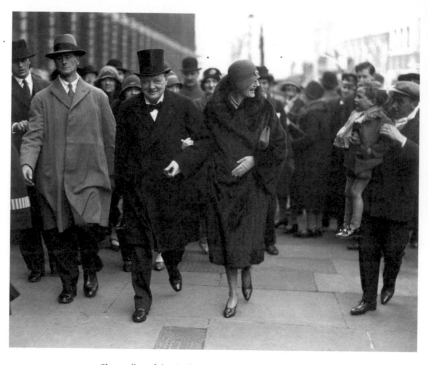

Chancellor of the Exchequer Winston Churchill and his
wife Clementine on their way to the House of Commons for the Budget.
15 April 1929

"It is a good thing for an uneducated man to
read books of quotations. ...
The quotations when engraved upon the
memory give you good thoughts."

On education at Bangalore, *My Early Life: A Roving Commission*, 1930.

"A baboon in a forest is a matter of legitimate speculation; a baboon in a zoo is an object of public curiosity; but a baboon in your wife's bed is a cause of the gravest concern."

On the growing German threat in the 1930s.

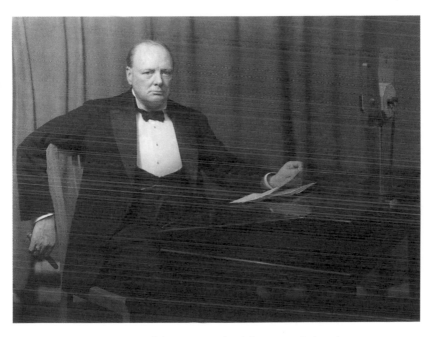

Conservative candidate Winston Churchill gives a radio broadcast while campaigning for Epping, Essex.
1 May 1929

"We know that he has, more than any other man, the gift of compressing the largest number of words into the smallest amount of thought."

On Ramsay MacDonald, speech on the European situation, House of Commons, 23 March 1933.

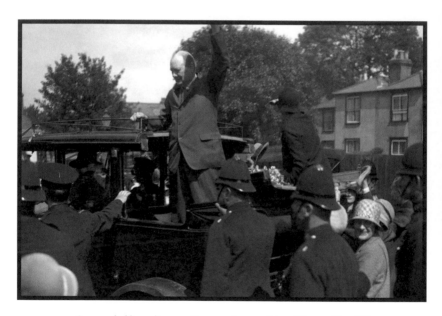

Surrounded by policemen, Conservative candidate Winston Churchill celebrates winning the Epping seat.
31 May 1929

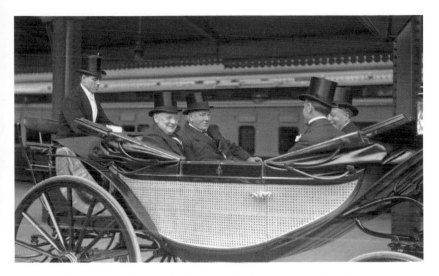

Winston Churchill (L) and Lord Cushendun leave Windsor station in a horse-drawn carriage.
7 June 1929

"One may dislike Hitler's system and yet admire his patriotic achievement. If our country were defeated, I hope we should find a champion as indomitable to restore our courage and lead us back to our place among the nations."

From 'Hitler and His Choice', published in
The Strand Magazine, November 1935.

"The Government simply cannot make up their mind, or they cannot get the Prime Minister to make up his mind. So they go on in strange paradox, decided only to be undecided, resolved to be irresolute, adamant for drift, solid for fluidity, all powerful to be impotent."

Speech criticizing Stanley Baldwin's government for its conciliatory stance towards Adolf Hitler.

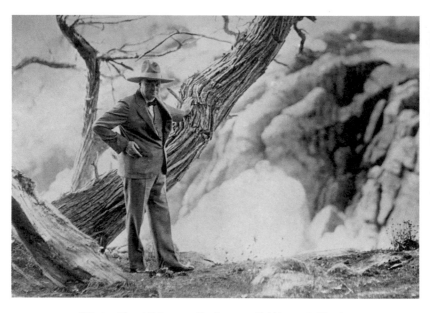

Winston Churchill, in ten-gallon hat, near Del Monte, California, during his visit to the Monterey Peninsula.
29 October 1929

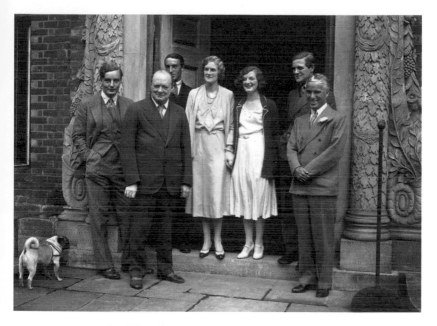

Winston Churchill and family during a visit to their home, Chartwell, near Westerham in Kent, by comedian and actor Charlie Chaplin (R).
1931

"Dictators ride to and fro on tigers from which they dare not dismount. And the tigers are getting hungry."

From 'Armistice – or Peace?', published in *The Evening Standard*,
11 November 1937.

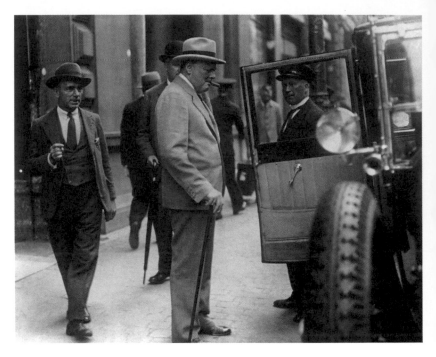

Winston Churchill during a visit to Brussels, Belgium.
1 September 1932

"Britain and France had to choose between war and dishonour. They chose dishonour. They will have war."

To Prime Minister Neville Chamberlain following the Munich Agreement,
House of Commons, 1938.

CHURCHILL IN QUOTES

"Death and sorrow will be the companions of our journey; hardship our garment; constancy and valour our only shield."

Speech, House of Commons, 8 October 1940.

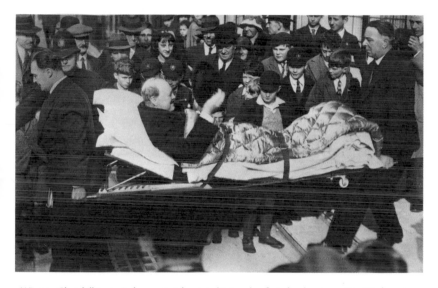

Winston Churchill is carried on a stretcher into his London flat after leaving a West End nursing home, where he had been suffering from paratyphoid.
10 October 1932

"The stations of uncensored expression are closing down; the lights are going out; but there is still time for those to whom freedom and parliamentary government mean something, to consult together. Let me, then, speak in truth and earnestness while time remains."

From 'The Defence of Freedom and Peace', radio broadcast
to the United States and London, 16 October 1938.

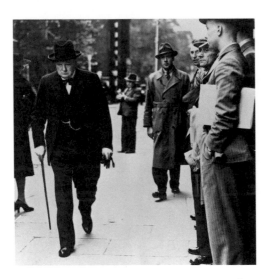

A grim-faced Winston Churchill leaves 10 Downing Street after visiting
Prime Minister Neville Chamberlain to discuss the Czech crisis.
10 September 1938

"I have nothing to offer but blood, toil, tears and sweat."

Speech after taking office as Prime Minister,
House of Commons, 13 May 1940.

"You ask, what is our policy?
I will say: It is to wage war, by sea, land and air, with all our might and with all the strength that God can give us: to wage war against a monstrous tyranny, never surpassed in the dark, lamentable catalogue of human crime. ...

... You ask, what is our aim? I can answer in one word: Victory, victory at all costs, victory in spite of all terror, victory, however long and hard the road may be; for without victory, there is no survival."

Speech after taking office as Prime Minister, House of Commons, 13 May 1940.

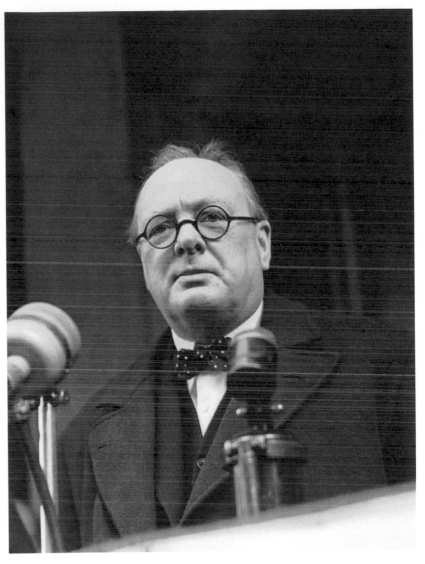

Winston Churchill addresses a recruiting meeting at the Mansion House,
London, during the build-up to the Second World War.
24 April 1939

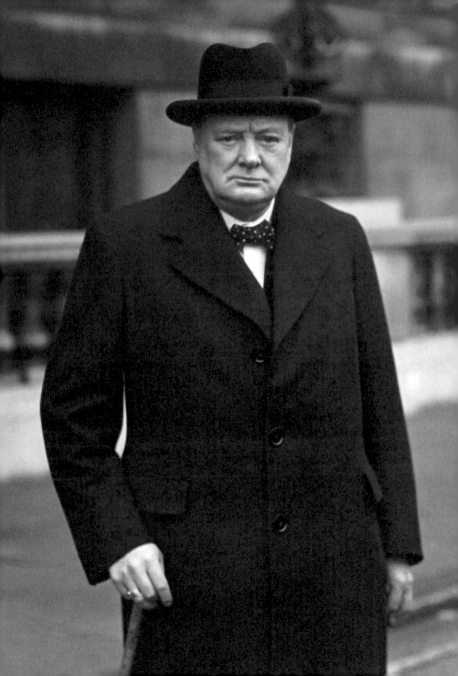

"We shall go on to the end, we shall fight in France, we shall fight on the seas and oceans, we shall fight ... in the air, we shall defend our Island, whatever the cost may be, we shall fight on the beaches, we shall fight on the landing grounds, we shall fight in the fields and in the streets, we shall fight in the hills; we shall never surrender..."

Speech following the evacuation of the British Expeditionary
Force from Dunkirk, House of Commons, 4 June 1940.

First Lord of the Admiralty
Winston Churchill on his way
to a War Council meeting.
14 October 1939

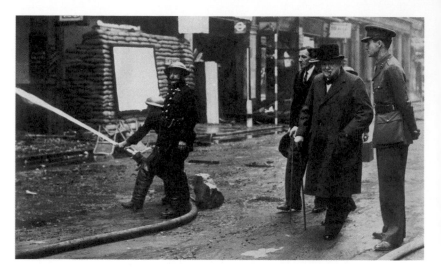

Prime Minister Winston Churchill surveys damage to the capital
inflicted by German bombers during the Blitz.
1 September 1940

"They remind me of the British squares at
Waterloo. They are not squares of soldiers;
they do not wear scarlet coats. They are
just ordinary English, Scottish and Welsh
folk: men, women and children standing
steadfastly together. But their spirit is the
same, their glory is the same; and,
in the end, their victory will be greater
than far-famed Waterloo."

Of Britain's bombed cities, radio broadcast, 9 February 1941.

"Bearing ourselves humbly before God ... we await undismayed the impending assault ... be the ordeal sharp or long, or both, we shall seek no terms, we shall tolerate no parlay; we may show mercy – we shall ask for none."

From 'War of the Unknown Warriors', broadcast on the BBC, 14 July 1940.

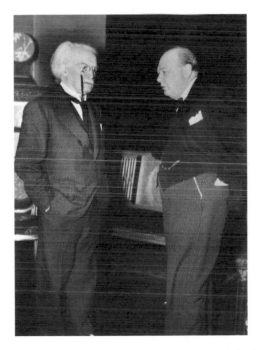

Prime Minister Winston Churchill talks with former Prime Minister David Lloyd George, who was in office throughout the First World War, during a lunch at the Chinese Embassy.
11 April 1941

"When I warned them that Britain would fight on alone whatever they did, their generals told their Prime Minister and his divided Cabinet, 'In three weeks, England will have her neck wrung like a chicken.' Some chicken! Some neck!"

On the French government, speech before Joint Session of the Canadian Parliament, Ottawa, 30 December 1941.

"We are waiting for the long-promised invasion. So are the fishes."

From '*Dieu Protège La France*' [God protect France], radio broadcast, 21 October 1940.

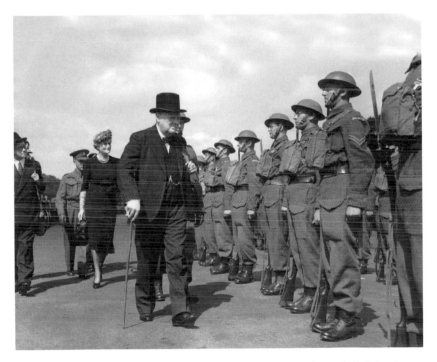

Prime Minister Winston Churchill inspects troops of the Home Guard in Hyde Park, London. 14 July 1941

"Goodnight then: sleep to gather strength for the morning. For the morning will come. Brightly will it shine on the brave and true, kindly upon all who suffer for the cause, glorious upon the tombs of heroes. Thus will shine the dawn. *Vive la France!*"

From '*Dieu Protège La France*' [God protect France], 21 October 1940.

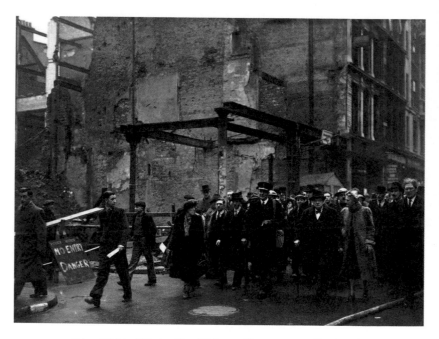

Prime Minister Winston Churchill (centre R), accompanied by his wife Clementine, tours the City of London after a German air raid.
30 December 1941

CHURCHILL IN QUOTES

"We will not say thereafter that the Greeks fight like heroes, but heroes fight like the Greeks!"

Statement after the news that the Greeks had repelled an attempted invasion by fascist Italy, December 1940.

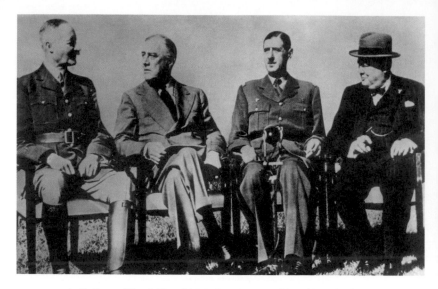

L–R: General Henri Giraud, High Commissioner of French North Africa;
US President Franklin D. Roosevelt; General Charles de Gaulle, leader of the Free French;
and Prime Minister Winston Churchill during a conference in Casablanca, Morocco.
14 January 1943

"Here is the answer which I will give to President Roosevelt: Put your confidence in us. ... We shall not fail or falter; we shall not weaken or tire. Neither the sudden shock of battle, nor the long-drawn trials of vigilance and exertion will wear us down. Give us the tools and we will finish the job."

BBC radio broadcast, 9 February 1941.

"If Hitler invaded Hell, I would make at least a favourable reference to the devil in the House of Commons."

To assistant private secretary John Colville on the eve of Operation Barbarossa, the German invasion of the Soviet Union, 21 June 1941.

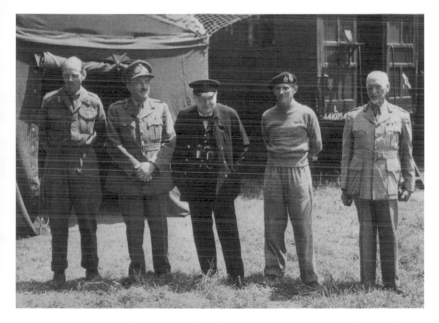

L–R: Lieutenant General Miles Dempsey, Field Marshal Sir Alan Brooke, Prime Minister Winston Churchill, General Bernard Law Montgomery and Field Marshal Jan Smuts of South Africa at the headquarters of 21st Army Group in southern England.
15 July 1943

"The terrible military machine – which we and the rest of the civilized world so foolishly, so supinely, so insensately allowed the Nazi gangsters to build up year by year from almost nothing – cannot stand idle lest it rust or fall to pieces. … So now this bloodthirsty guttersnipe must launch his mechanized armies upon new fields of slaughter, pillage and devastation."

Radio broadcast on the German invasion of the Soviet Union, 22 June 1941.

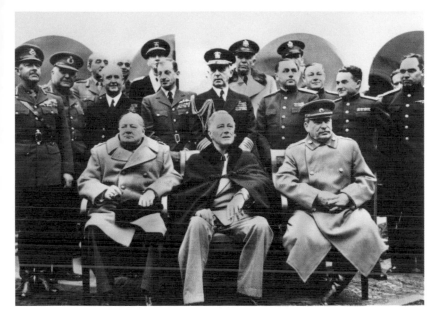

L–R: Winston Churchill, US President Franklin D. Roosevelt and Soviet leader Josef Stalin with their advisors at Yalta, in the Crimea, where the Allies decided the future of post-war Europe. 4 February 1945

"It is a mistake to look too far ahead. Only one link in the chain of destiny can be handled at a time."

Speech following the Yalta conference with US President Franklin D. Roosevelt and Soviet General Secretary Joseph Stalin, House of Commons, 27 February 1945.

"'In war-time,' I said, 'truth is so precious she should always be attended by a bodyguard of lies.'"

Discussion of Operation Overlord with Stalin at the Teheran Conference, 30 November 1943, cited in *The Second World War, Volume V: Closing the Ring*, 1952.

"Of course, when you are winning a war almost everything that happens can be claimed to be right and wise."

The Second World War, Volume V: Closing the Ring, 1952.

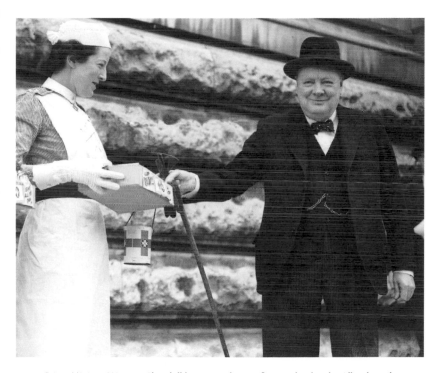

Prime Minister Winston Churchill buys a Red Cross flag on the day the Allies launch their invasion of mainland Europe with Operation Overlord.
6 June 1944

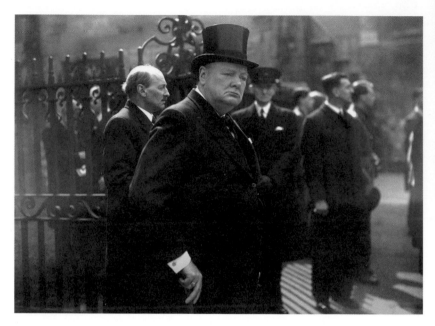

Prime Minister Winston Churchill leaves Westminster Abbey, London, after a memorial
service in honour of former Prime Minister David Lloyd George.
April 1945

"I am never going to have anything more
to do with politics or politicians. When
this war is over, I shall confine myself
entirely to writing and painting."

"Meeting Roosevelt was like uncorking your first bottle of champagne."

Reflecting on his relationship with Franklin D. Roosevelt during a visit to the President's grave in Hyde Park, New York, 12 March 1946.

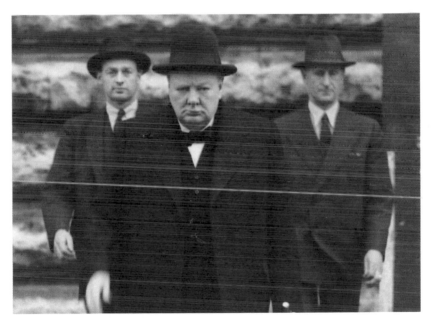

Winston Churchill on his way to the House of Commons to pay tribute
to US President Franklin D. Roosevelt who had died that day.
12 April 1945

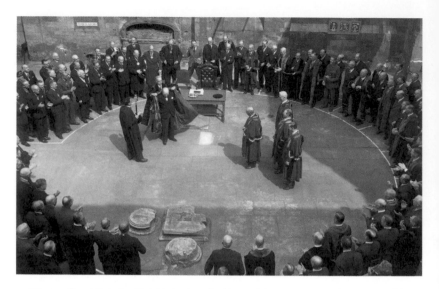

Winston Churchill during his initiation into the Mercers' Company among the remains of the Mercers' Hall, which had been destroyed by fire during an air raid.
25 April 1945

"Let me have the best solution worked out. Don't argue the matter. The difficulties will argue for themselves."

Memo, of 30 May 1942, to the Chief of Combined Operations on the design of floating piers (Mulberry Harbours) for use on landing beaches, cited in *The Second World War, Volume V: Closing the Ring,* 1952.

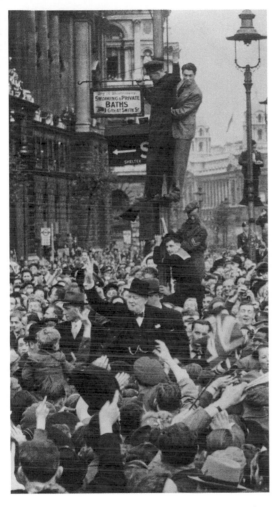

"Now this is not the end. It is not even the beginning of the end. But it is, perhaps, the end of the beginning."

Referring to the British victory over the Germans at El Alamein in Egypt, speech during Lord Mayor's Luncheon, Mansion House, 10 November 1942.

Prime Minister Winston Churchill is mobbed by excited crowds as he travels to the House of Commons following his victory speech from the balcony of the Ministry of Health on VE Day.
8 May 1945

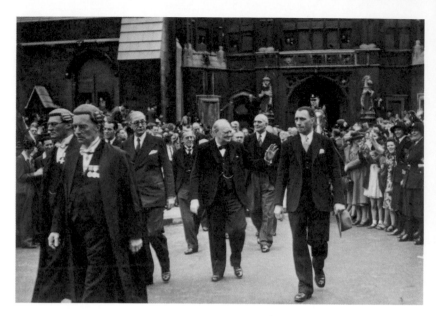

Prime Minister Winston Churchill waves to the waiting crowd as he leaves the House of Commons following the news of the defeat of Germany (Victory in Europe day).
8 May 1945

"The maxim 'Nothing avails but perfection' may be spelt shorter: 'Paralysis.'"

Note to General Ismay on proposed improvements to landing craft,
6 December 1942.

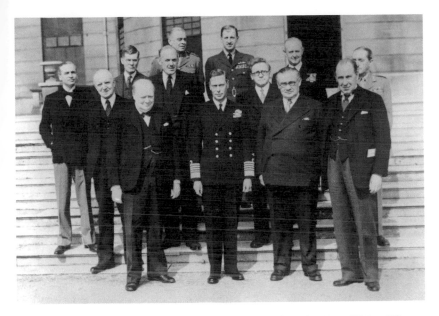

King George VI (C) with members of the wartime Cabinet. To his right is Prime Minister Winston
Churchill, and to his left, Minister of Labour Ernest Bevin.
10 May 1945

"By its sudden collapse ... the proud German army has once again proved the truth of the saying, 'The Hun is always either at your throat or at your feet.'"

Speech before Joint Session of Congress, Washington, DC, 19 May 1943.

"To achieve the extirpation of Nazi tyranny, there are no lengths of violence to which we will not go."

Speech, House of Commons, 21 September 1943.

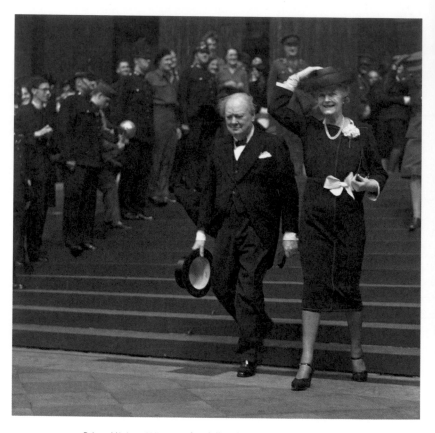

Prime Minister Winston Churchill and his wife Clementine leave
St Paul's Cathedral after a Victory Thanksgiving Service.
13 May 1945

"When the war of the giants is over, the wars of the pygmies will begin."

From a telegram to US President Franklin D. Roosevelt, 18 March 1945.

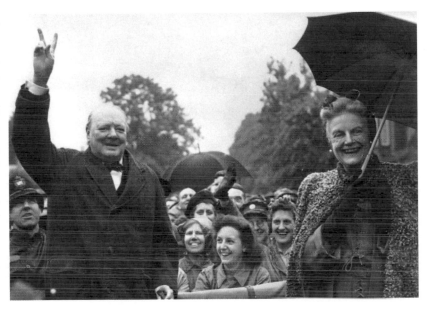

Winston Churchill with his wife Clementine campaigning at Loughton in his
Essex constituency. Churchill is giving his famous victory sign.
26 June 1945

"By noon it was clear that the Socialists would have a majority. At luncheon my wife said to me, 'It may well be a blessing in disguise.' I replied, 'At the moment it seems quite effectively disguised.'"

On the 26 July 1945 landslide electoral defeat that turned him out of office, cited in *The Second World War, Volume VI: Triumph and Tragedy*, 1954.

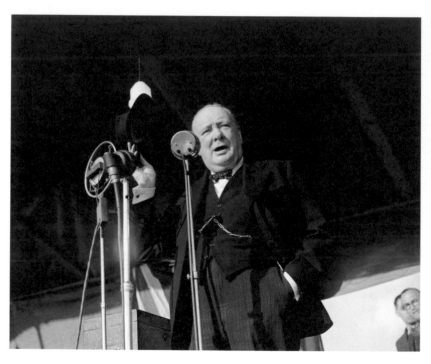

Prime Minister Winston Churchill gives his final election address to an audience of over 20,000 at Walthamstow Stadium, London.
4 July 1945

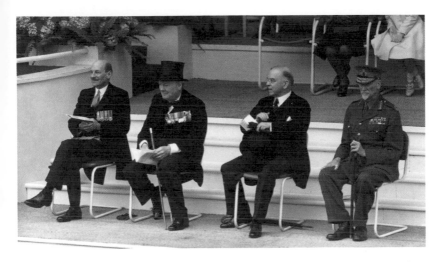

Winston Churchill (second L) and newly elected Prime Minister Clement Attlee (L), among other dignitaries, watch a military parade during the official victory celebrations in London.
8 June 1946

"From Stettin in the Baltic to Trieste in the Adriatic, an iron curtain has descended across the Continent."

Speech on Soviet communism and the Cold War, Fulton, Missouri, 5 March 1946.

"Never give in – never, never, never, never, in nothing great or small, large or petty, never give in except to convictions of honour and good sense. Never yield to force; never yield to the apparently overwhelming might of the enemy."

Speech, Harrow School, 29 October 1941.

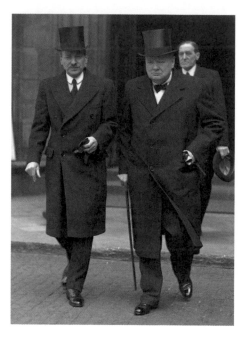

Prime Minister Clement Attlee (L) and Winston Churchill leave Westminster Abbey in London after attending a memorial service for Field Marshal Lord Gort.
18 April 1946

"In attack most daring, in defence most cunning, in endurance most steadfast, they performed a feat of arms which will be remembered and recounted as long as the virtues of courage and resolution have power to move the hearts of men."

On the First Airborne Division at Arnhem, Netherlands, 1944.

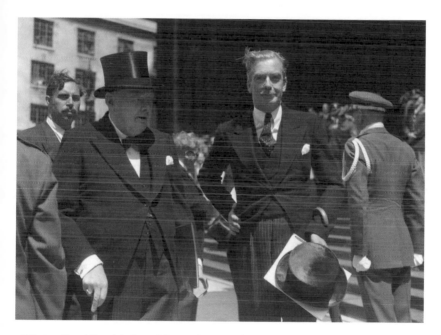

Winston Churchill and Anthony Eden on the steps of St Paul's Cathedral after General Dwight Eisenhower had presented a roll of honour bearing the names of 28,000 Americans killed in or operating from Great Britain during the Second World War.
4 July 1946

"This is Winston Churchill speaking. If you have a microphone in my room, it is a waste of time. I do not talk in my sleep."

During a visit to the Soviet Union, when told his room may have been bugged.

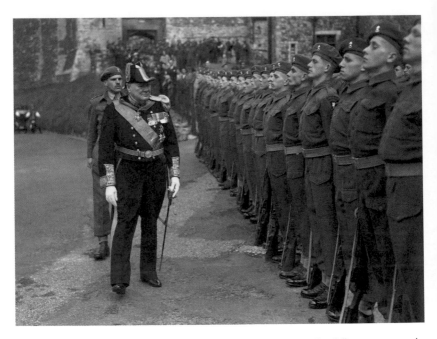

Dressed in his uniform of Lord Warden of the Cinque Ports, Winston Churchill inspects a guard of honour from the 4th Coast Training Regiment Royal Artillery at Dover Castle.
14 August 1946

"I felt as if I were walking with destiny, and that all my past life had been but a preparation for this hour and for this trial."

On his appointment as Prime Minister on 10 May 1940, *The Second World War, Volume I: The Gathering Storm*, 1948.

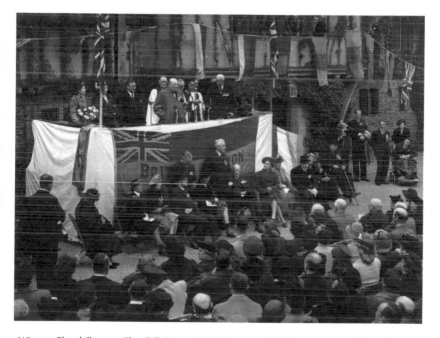

Winston Churchill opens Churchill Court, a British Legion rehabilitation centre and convalescent home near Sevenoaks, Kent, for men who served during the Second World War.
12 October 1946

"Bessie, my dear, you are ugly, and what's more, you are disgustingly ugly. But tomorrow I shall be sober and you will still be disgustingly ugly."

In response to MP Bessie Braddock, who had chastised Churchill for being "disgustingly drunk", 1946.

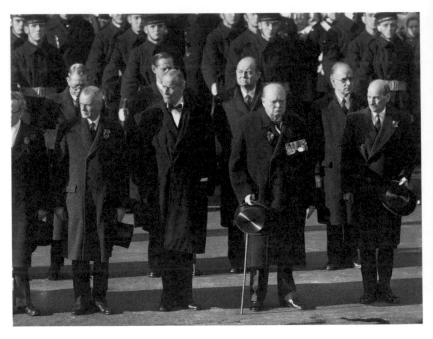

Prime Minister Clement Attlee (R), Winston Churchill (second R) and other leading politicians observe the Two Minutes' Silence at the Cenotaph on Remembrance Day.
10 November 1946

"I had been brought up and trained to have the utmost contempt for people who got drunk – and I would have liked to have the boozing scholars of the Universities wheeled into line and properly chastised for their squalid misuse of what I must ever regard as a gift of the gods."

On the Malakand Field Force, *My Early Life: A Roving Commission*, 1930.

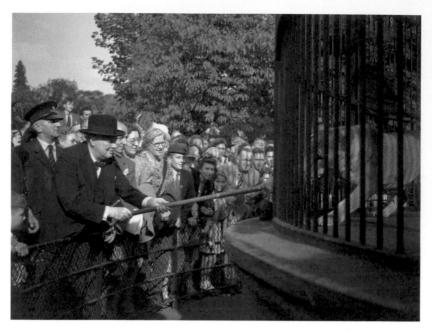

Winston Churchill feeds his lion, Rota, at London Zoo. Rota had been kept
as a cub at a house in Pinner, Middlesex, but when he grew too large,
he was presented to Churchill and housed in Regent's Park.
10 September 1947

It was the nation and the race dwelling
all round the globe that had the lion's heart.
I had the luck to be called upon to give the
roar. I also hope that I sometimes suggested
to the lion the right place to use his claws.

Speech at his eightieth birthday celebration, Westminster Hall, 30 November 1954

Many forms of government have been tried and will be tried in this world of sin and woe. No one pretends that democracy is perfect or all-wise. Indeed, it has been said that democracy is the worst form of government except all those other forms that have been tried from time to time.

Speech, House of Commons, 11 November 1947.

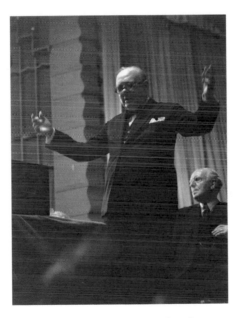

Leader of the Opposition Winston Churchill emphasizes a point during a speech at the Conservative Party Conference in Brighton. 4 October 1947

"For my part, I consider that it will be found much better by all parties to leave the past to history, especially as I propose to write that history."

Speech, House of Commons, 23 January 1948.

"Madam, all babies look like me."

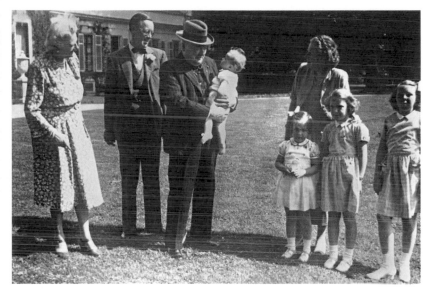

Winston Churchill and his wife Clementine (L) with Prince Bernhard of the Netherlands,
Princess Juliana and their children. Churchill was in The Netherlands
for the opening of the Congress of Europe.
10 May 1948

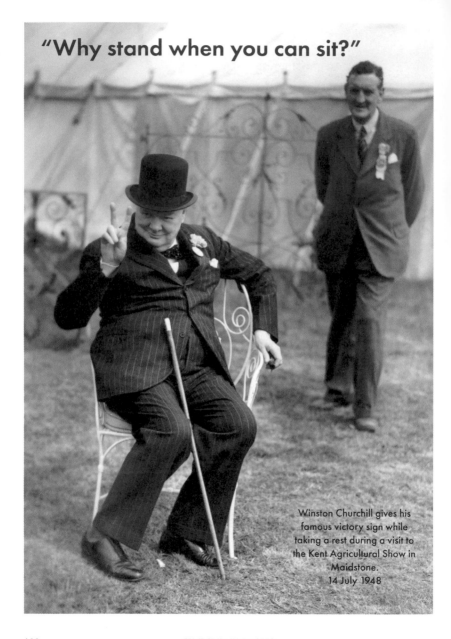

"Why stand when you can sit?"

Winston Churchill gives his famous victory sign while taking a rest during a visit to the Kent Agricultural Show in Maidstone.
14 July 1948

"Broadly speaking, short words are best, and the old words, when short, are best of all."

Speech on receiving *The Times* Literary Award,
2 November 1949.

"The reason for having diplomatic relations is not to confer a compliment, but to secure a convenience."

Speech on diplomatic recognition of the People's Republic of China, House of Commons, 17 November 1949.

"I cannot pretend to feel impartial about the colours. I rejoice with the brilliant ones, and am genuinely sorry for the poor browns."

From 'Painting as a Pastime', published in *The Strand Magazine*, December 1921 / January 1922.

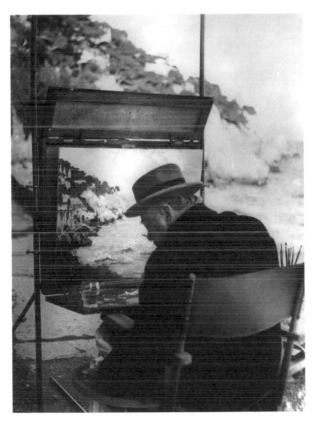

Winston Churchill painting in Monte Carlo.
1 September 1949

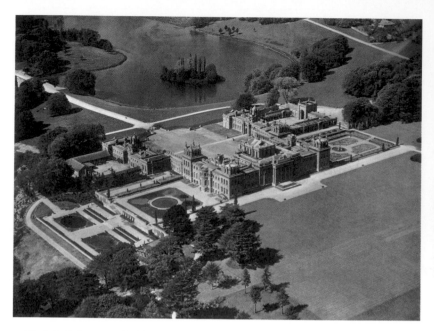

Blenheim Palace in Oxfordshire, seat of the Dukes of Marlborough, and the birthplace and ancestral home of Winston Churchill.
1950

"At Blenheim, I took two very important decisions: to be born and to marry. I am content with the decision I took on both occasions."

"He has all the virtues I dislike and none of the vices I admire."

On Labour politician Sir Stafford Cripps.

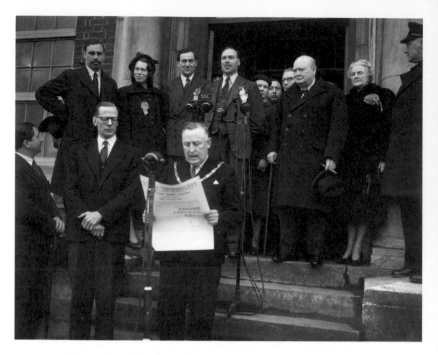

Winston Churchill smiles as the Mayor of Woodford declares his 18,499
majority over his Labour opponent in the General Election.
24 February 1950

"War is mainly a catalogue of blunders."

**On the Soviet Union's failure to form a united Balkan front against
Hitler, *The Second World War, Volume III: The Grand Alliance*, 1950.**

"A communist is like a crocodile: when it opens its mouth, you cannot tell whether it is trying to smile or preparing to eat you up."

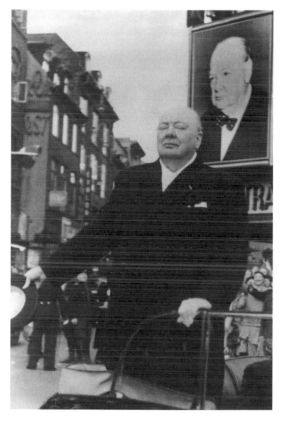

In front of a giant portrait of himself, Winston Churchill waves to the Danish public as he tours Copenhagen. During his drive through the city, communists threw leaflets at him.
10 October 1950

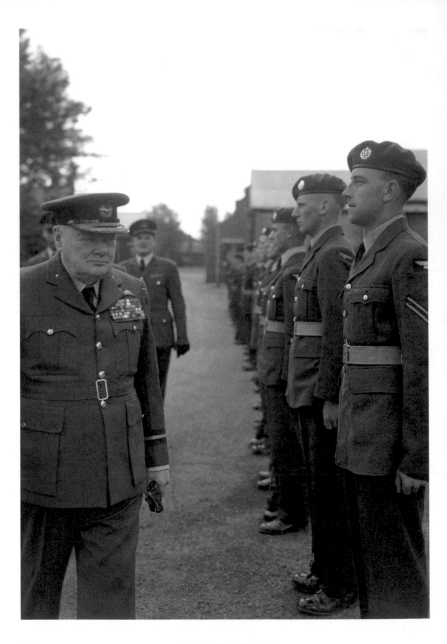

"The gratitude of every home in our Island, in our Empire, and indeed throughout the world ... goes out to the British airmen who, undaunted by odds, unwearied in their constant challenge and mortal danger, are turning the tide of the World War by their prowess and by their devotion. Never in the field of human conflict was so much owed by so many to so few."

Speech in praise of the Royal Air Force during the Battle of Britain, House of Commons, 20 August 1940.

Wearing his air commodore's uniform, Winston Churchill inspects the guard of honour during a visit to 615 (County of Surrey) Squadron, Royal Auxiliary Air Force, at Biggin Hill, Kent. 18 June 1951

"I think I can save the British Empire from anything – except the British."

On the British intellectuals and their severe criticisms of Britain.

"I am not usually accused even by my friends of being of a modest or retiring disposition."

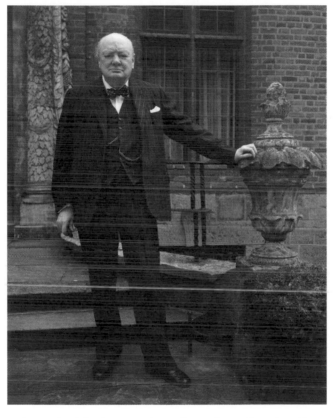

Winston Churchill at his country home, Chartwell, near Westerham, Kent, ready to lead the Conservative Party's campaign for the General Election called by Clement Attlee.
20 September 1951

"I drink and smoke and I am two hundred per cent fit."

In reply to Field Marshal Viscount Montgomery, who had said, "I neither drink nor smoke and am a hundred per cent fit."

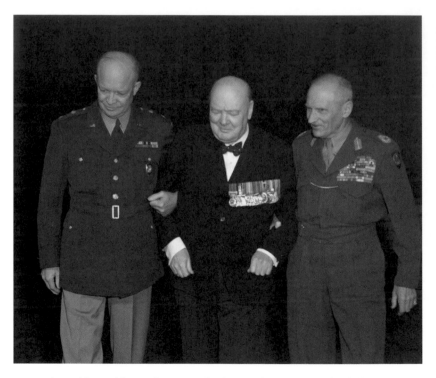

Three of the world's most famous war leaders march arm in arm at the El Alamein Reunion at Earls Court, London. L–R: US General Dwight D. Eisenhower, Winston Churchill and Field Marshal Viscount Montgomery of Alamein.
19 October 1951

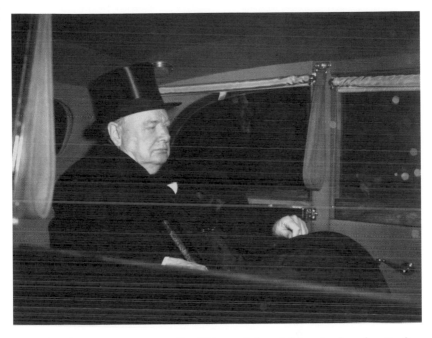

A grim-faced Prime Minister Winston Churchill leaves St James's Palace, London, after attending
a Privy Council meeting, summoned upon the death of King George VI.
6 February 1952

"It's not enough that we do our best;
sometimes we have to do what's required."

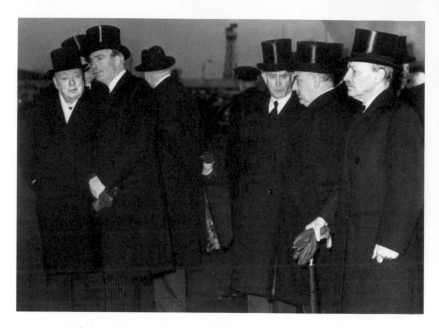

L–R: Prime Minister Winston Churchill, Foreign Secretary Anthony Eden,
Liberal leader Clement Davies, Home Secretary Sir David Maxwell Fyfe and Leader
of the Opposition Clement Attlee await the aircraft returning Princess Elizabeth
from Kenya following the death of her father, the King.
6 February 1952

"Plans are of little importance, but planning is essential."

"Continuous effort – not strength or intelligence – is the key to unlocking our potential."

"There are two things that are more difficult than making an after-dinner speech: climbing a wall which is leaning toward you and kissing a girl who is leaning away from you."

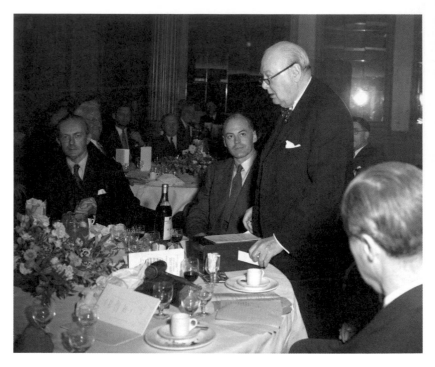

Guest of honour Prime Minister Winston Churchill speaks at the Press Association lunch at the Savoy Hotel, London. The lunch was held in conjunction with the PA's eighty-fourth Annual General Meeting.
11 June 1952

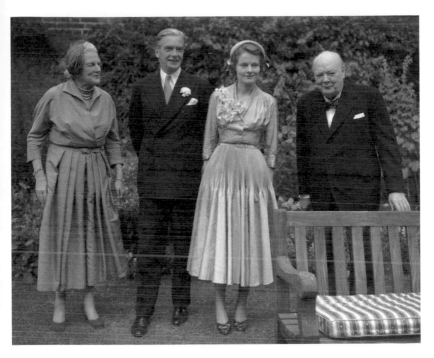

Prime Minister Winston Churchill and his wife Clementine in the garden of
10 Downing Street with Foreign Secretary Anthony Eden
and his new bride, Clarissa, Churchill's niece.
14 August 1952

When I am abroad, I always make
it a rule never to criticize or attack the
government of my country. I make up
for lost time when I am at home.

Speech, House of Commons,
18 April 1947.

"Without tradition, art is a flock of sheep without a shepherd.
Without innovation, it is a corpse."

Speech at the Royal Academy of Art, 1953.

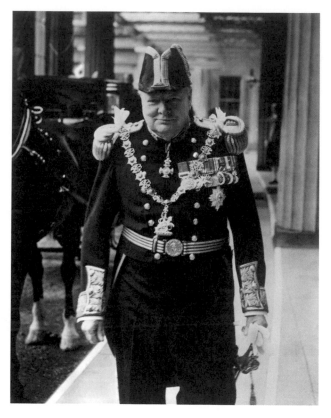

Dressed in his uniform as Lord Warden of the Cinque Ports, with his Order of the Garter insignia (the Great George) around his neck, Prime Minister Winston Churchill leaves Buckingham Palace for the procession of Prime Ministers to attend the Queen's Coronation at Westminster Abbey.
2 June 1953

"I am easily satisfied with the best."

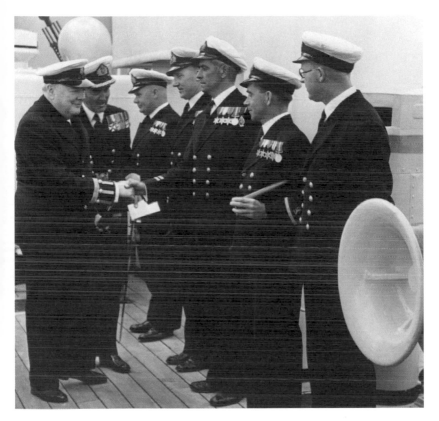

Prime Minister Winston Churchill, in the uniform of an Elder Brother of Trinity House, is introduced to the officers of the Trinity House vessel Patricia prior to taking part in the Coronation Naval Review at Spithead in the Solent.
15 June 1953

"There is no such thing as public opinion. There is only published opinion."

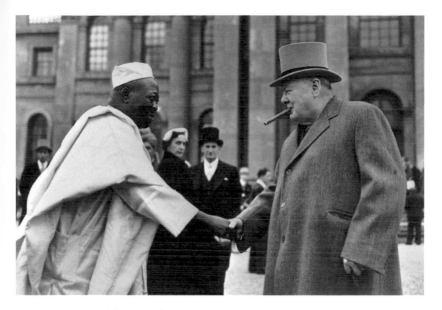

The Ooni (king) of Ife, Oba Adesoji Aderemi II, shakes hands with Prime Minister Winston
Churchill during a garden party at Blenheim Palace.
1953

"Writing a book is an adventure. To begin
with, it is a toy and an amusement; then it
becomes a mistress, and then it becomes a
master, and then a tyrant. The last phase is
that just as you are about to be reconciled
to your servitude, you kill the monster, and
fling him out to the public."

"The price of greatness is responsibility."

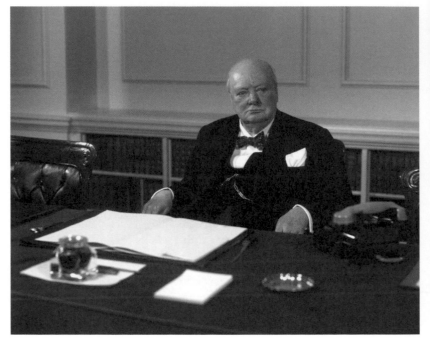

Prime Minister Sir Winston Churchill in the Cabinet Room at 10 Downing Street.
1954

"Every day you may make progress. Every step may be fruitful. Yet there will stretch out before you an ever-lengthening, ever-ascending, ever-improving path. You know you will never get to the end of the journey. But this, so far from discouraging, only adds to the joy and the glory of the climb."

From 'Painting as a Pastime', published in *The Strand Magazine*, December 1921 / January 1922.

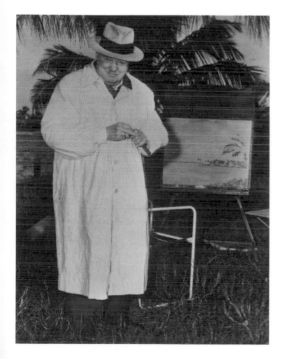

Prime Minister Sir Winston Churchill takes a break from his painting to pose for the camera while on holiday in Florida. 3 February 1954

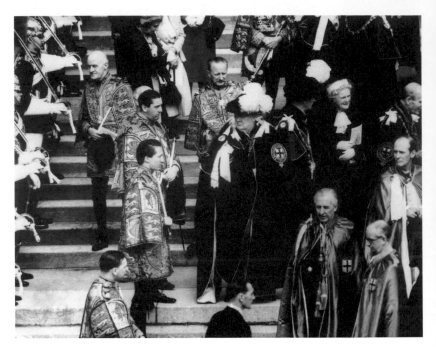

Sir Winston Churchill (C, in robes) outside St George's Chapel, Windsor,
after his installation as a Knight of the Garter.
14 June 1954

"To jaw-jaw is always better than to war-war."

Remarks at a White House luncheon, 6 June 1954.

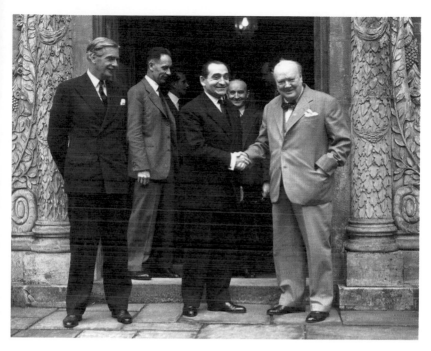

Prime Minister Sir Winston Churchill shakes hands with French Prime Minister Pierre Mendes France during the latter's visit to Chartwell. Foreign Secretary Anthony Eden (L) looks on.
23 August 1954

"Some people's idea of [free speech]
is that they are free to say what they like,
but if anyone says anything back,
that is an outrage."

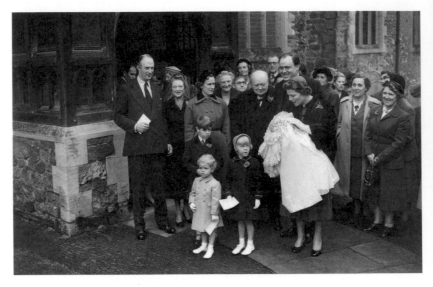

Sir Winston Churchill (C) in a family group photographed at the christening
of his granddaughter, Charlotte Clementine Soames.
6 November 1954

"For myself, I am an optimist – it does not seem to be much use being anything else."

Speech at Lord Mayor's Banquet, London, 9 November 1954.

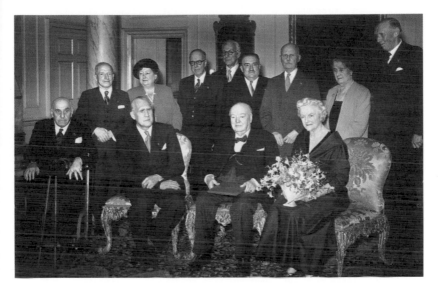

The British Legion presents a birthday gift to Prime Minister Sir Winston Churchill.
Front row (L–R): Sir Brunel Cohen, Sir Ian Fraser, Sir Winston and Lady Churchill.
Dame Regina Evans stands behind Lady Churchill.
24 November 1954

"Personally I'm always ready to learn, although I do not always like being taught."

"Difficulties mastered are opportunities won."

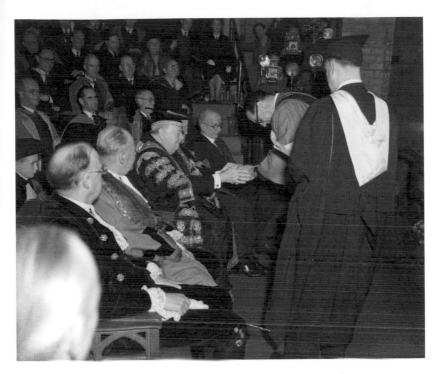

Sir Winston Churchill confers the Honorary Degree of Doctor of Laws
upon Sir Walter Monckton at Bristol University.
26 November 1954

"The empires of the future are the empires of the mind."

Speech at Harvard University, 6 September 1943.

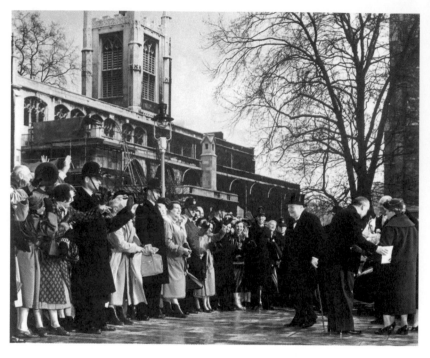

Prime Minister Sir Winston Churchill greets the crowds at Westminster, London.
30 November 1954

"We shape our buildings, and afterwards our buildings shape us."

Speech on rebuilding the Chamber of the House of Commons (destroyed by a German bomb on 10 May 1941), House of Commons, 28 October 1943.

CHURCHILL IN QUOTES

"An appeaser is one who feeds a crocodile – hoping it will eat him last."

Cited in *Reader's Digest*, December 1954.

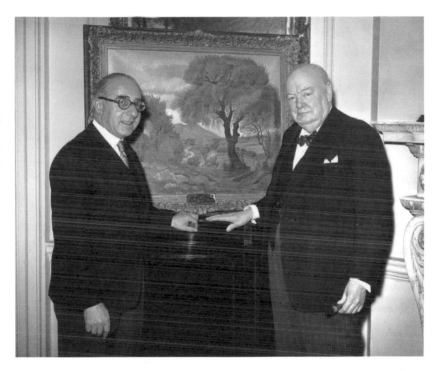

Argentine Ambassador Dr Domingo Derisi presents a painting by Lino Spilimbergo to Prime Minister Sir Winston Churchill as a gift to celebrate his eightieth birthday.
9 December 1954

"I'm just preparing my impromptu remarks."

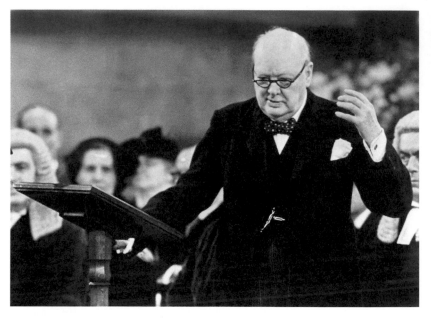

Prime Minister Sir Winston Churchill speaks after receiving an illuminated book containing the signatures of all members of both Houses of Parliament to commemorate his eightieth birthday at Westminster Hall, London.
30 December 1954

"You have enemies?
Good. That means
you've stood up for
something, sometime
in your life."

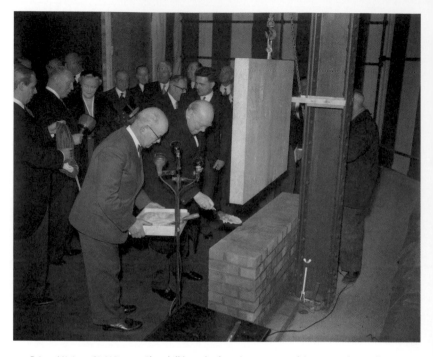

Prime Minister Sir Winston Churchill lays the foundation stone of the new Baltic Exchange building in London. As a man who had made bricklaying his hobby, he was able to state that the stone was well and truly laid.
22 March 1955

"The day may dawn when fair play, love for one's fellow men, respect for justice and freedom, will enable tormented generations to march forth triumphant from the hideous epoch in which we have to dwell. Meanwhile, never flinch, never weary, never despair."

From his last major speech in the House of Commons, 1 March 1955.

"My idea of a good dinner is, first to have good food, then discuss good food, and after this good food has been elaborately discussed, to discuss a good topic – with me as chief conversationalist."

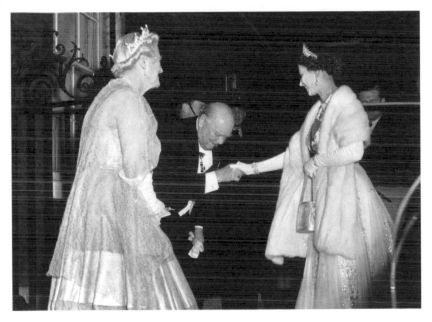

Watched by Lady Churchill, Prime Minister Sir Winston Churchill bows to Queen Elizabeth II as he welcomes her and the Duke of Edinburgh to 10 Downing Street for dinner.
4 April 1955

"Criticism may not be agreeable, but it is necessary. It fulfils the same function as pain in the human body. It calls attention to an unhealthy state of things."

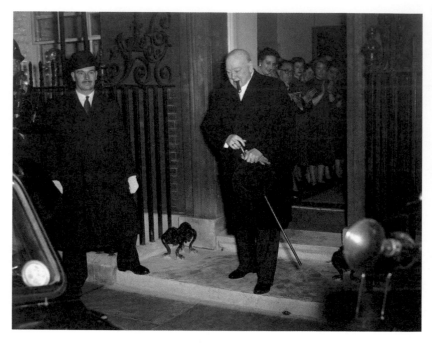

Members of staff applaud as Sir Winston Churchill leaves
10 Downing Street after resigning as Prime Minister.
6 April 1955

CHURCHILL IN QUOTES

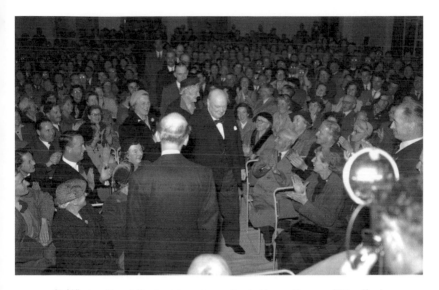

Sir Winston Churchill enjoys a great reception in his constituency of Woodford,
Essex, during his General Election campaign.
16 May 1955

"Dogs look up to you, cats look down on
you. Give me a pig! He looks you in the eye
and treats you as an equal."

"I want no criticism of America at my table. The Americans criticize themselves more than enough."

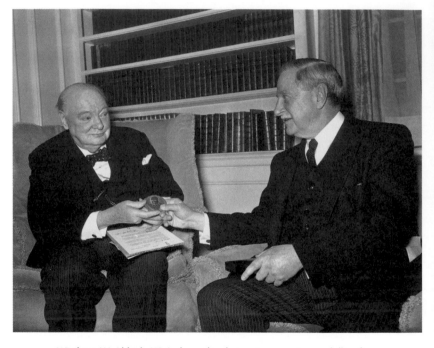

Winthrop W. Aldrich, US Ambassador-designate, presents a medallion from President Dwight D. Eisenhower to Sir Winston Churchill. The medallion had been struck specially to commemorate his eighty-first birthday.
30 November 1955

"When I was younger, I made it a rule never to take strong drink before lunch. It is now my rule never to do so before breakfast."

To King George VI, on a cold morning at the airport, after the King had asked if Churchill would take something to warm himself.

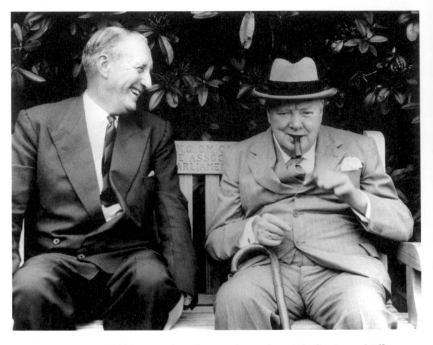

Sir Winston Churchill shares a joke with General Sir Lashmer Whistler, General Officer
Commanding of the Army's Western Command.
19 December 1955

"One does not leave a convivial party before closing time."

"Eating my own words has never given me indigestion."

"When I was a young subaltern in the South African War, the water was not fit to drink. To make it palatable, we had to put a bit of whisky in it. By diligent effort, I learned to like it.'

During an exchange with US President Harry S. Truman aboard the Presidential train, Washington, DC, 4 March 1946.

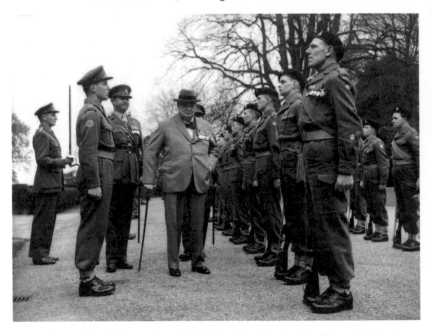

Sir Winston Churchill inspects men of the Cinque Ports Battalion Royal Sussex Regiment, which was visiting him at his home, Chartwell, near Westerham, Kent. Sir Winston was Honorary Colonel of the Territorial Army unit. 30 April 1956

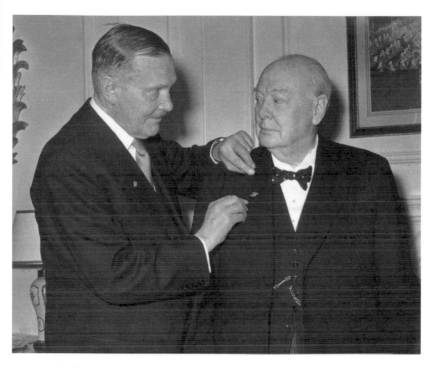

New Zealander Lord Freyberg presents the New Zealand Returned Services Association Gold Badge to Sir Winston Churchill at his home in Hyde Park Gate, London. The association is New Zealand's equivalent of the British Legion, and the badge its highest honour.
8 May 1957

"I must warn him that he runs a very grave risk of falling into senility before he is overtaken by age."

Interruption to an MP's rambling speech against his wartime policies.

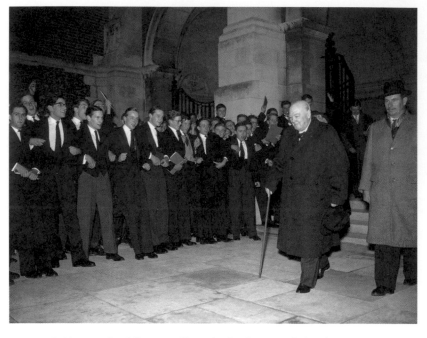

Sir Winston Churchill is greeted by ranks of enthusiastic scholars during a visit
to his old school, Harrow, for the annual Songs Concert.
25 October 1957

"Headmasters have powers at their disposal with which Prime Ministers have never yet been invested."

On schooling at Harrow, *My Early Life: A Roving Commission*, 1930.

"Yes, now bugger off."

In reply to his grandson, who had asked if he was the greatest man living.

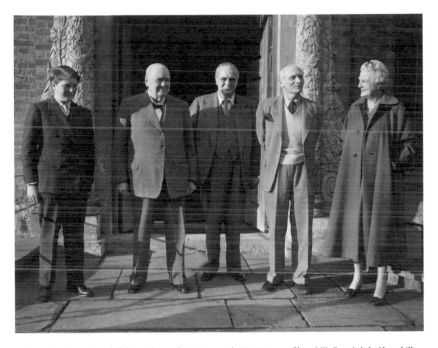

L–R: Winston Churchill (grandson of Sir Winston), Sir Winston Churchill, Randolph Churchill (son of Sir Winston), Field Marshal Viscount Montgomery and Lady Churchill, pictured at Chartwell on Sir Winston's eighty-third birthday.
30 November 1957

"... I pity undergraduates, when I see what frivolous lives many of them lead in the midst of precious fleeting opportunity. After all, a man's Life must be nailed to a cross either of Thought or Action. Without work there is no play."

On education at Bangalore, *My Early Life: A Roving Commission*, 1930.

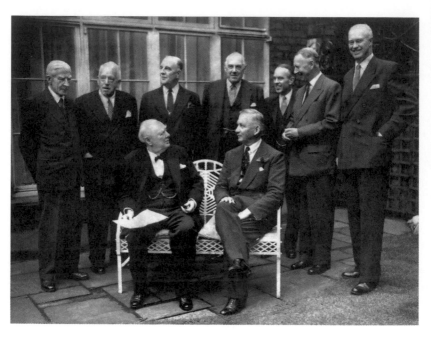

Sir Winston Churchill (seated, L) with trustees of the proposed Churchill College at Cambridge University. Seated beside him is Lord Tedder. Standing (L–R): Lord Adrian, Sir Alexander Fleck, Lord Godber, Viscount Chandos, J. R. Colville (not a trustee), Lord Knollys (not a trustee) and Professor Sir Alexander Todd.
15 June 1958

"He looks like a female llama who has been surprised in the bath."

On Charles de Gaulle.

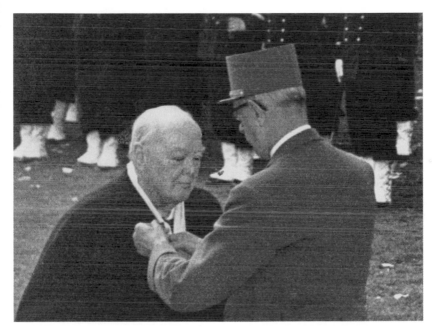

Sir Winston Churchill receives the Cross of Liberation from General Charles de Gaulle in the grounds of the Hôtel Matignon, Paris.
7 November 1958

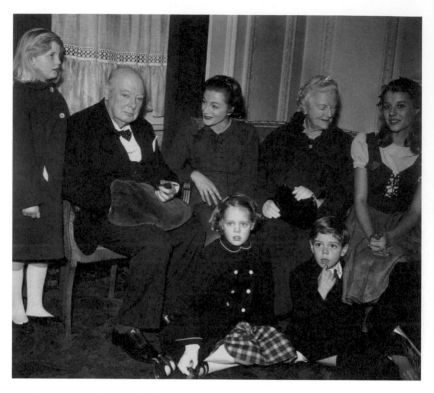

Sir Winston and Lady Churchill with their actress daughter Sarah (C) and three of their grandchildren, Arabella (L), Emma and Jeremy Soames after attending a performance of *Peter Pan*, in which Sarah played Peter Pan. At right is Julia Lockwood, who played Wendy. 30 December 1958

"Play the game for more than you can afford to lose ... only then will you learn the game."

"There is less there than meets the eye."

On Prime Minister Clement Attlee to President Truman, 1946.

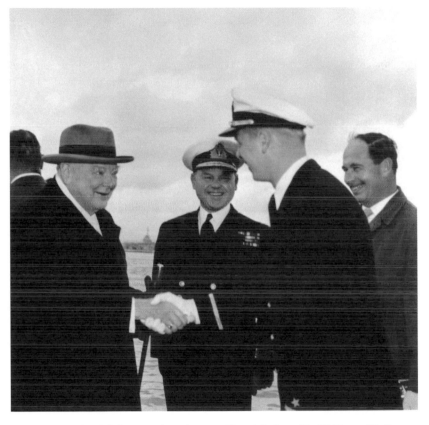

Sir Winston Churchill shares a joke with Ensign Glenn J. Sedam of the US Navy while Rear Admiral D. F. Powlett, Flag Officer Commanding at Gibraltar, looks on. Sedam, of the USS *Northampton*, was visiting Gibraltar after exercises in the Mediterranean.
5 March 1959

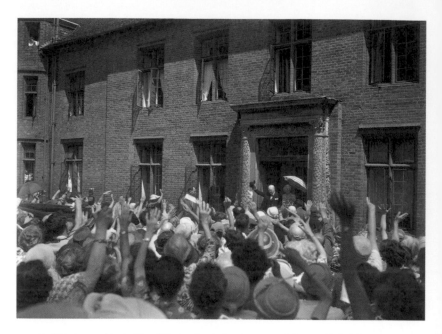

Sir Winston and Lady Churchill, standing in the doorway of Chartwell, their home near Westerham in Kent, wave to a crowd of visitors who were there after the grounds had been opened to the public in aid of two local parish churches.
8 July 1959

"One must regard the hyphen as a blemish to be avoided whenever possible."

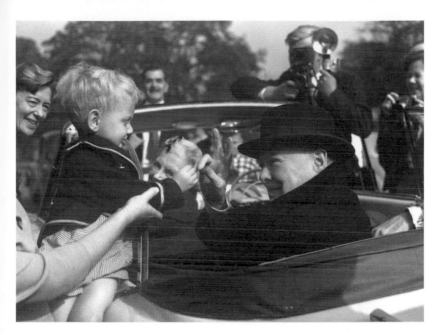

Mrs McArthur holds her son Andrew (3) as Sir Winston Churchill gives him his famous
victory sign while driving through his constituency of Woodford in Essex.
8 October 1959

"There is no finer investment for any
community than putting milk into babies."

Radio broadcast, 21 March 1943.

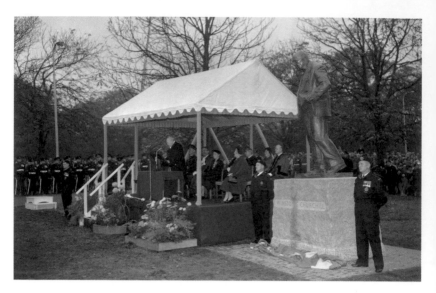

Sir Winston Churchill speaks after a bronze statue of him had been unveiled by Field Marshal Viscount Montgomery at Salway Hill, in Churchill's constituency of Woodford, Essex. The 8ft 6in statue was sculpted by David McFall.
31 October 1959

"No folly is more costly than the folly of intolerant idealism."

"Like chasing a quinine pill around a cow pasture."

On the game of golf

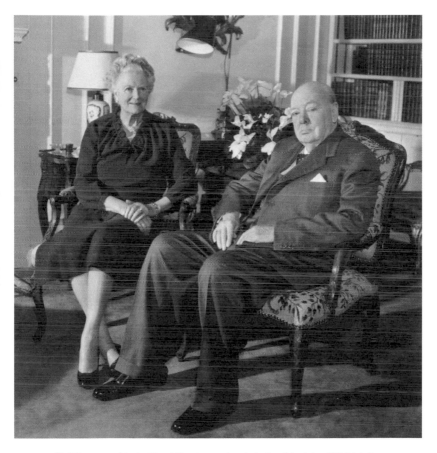

Sir Winston and Lady Churchill at home shortly before his eighty-fifth birthday.
28 November 1959

"I like a man who grins when he fights."

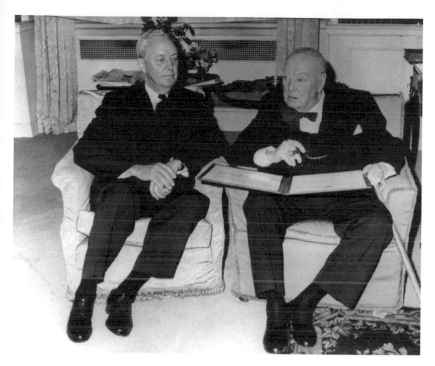

Sir Winston Churchill holds a copy of the Proclamation declaring his Honorary American Citizenship presented by US Ambassador David Bruce at his London home. The Proclamation was read by President Kennedy during a ceremony at the White House, Washington, where Sir Winston was represented by his son, Randolph.
12 April 1963

"This Treasury paper, by its very length, defends itself against the risk of being read."

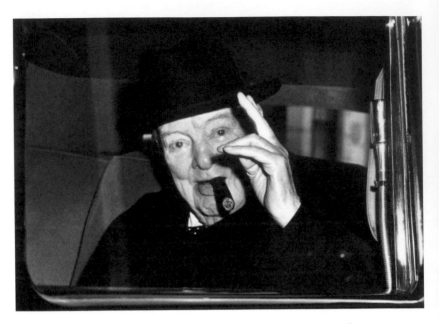

Sir Winston Churchill waves from his car while on his way to the House of Commons, Westminster, on the day that *The Finest Hours*, a film based on his life, was premiered in London. 29 April 1964

"The greatest lesson in life is to know that even fools are right sometimes."

"A fanatic is one who can't change his mind and won't change the subject."

"Let us therefore brace ourselves to our duties, and so bear ourselves that, if the British Empire and its Commonwealth last for a thousand years, men will still say, 'This was their finest hour.'"

Speech on the war situation, House of Commons,
18 June 1940.

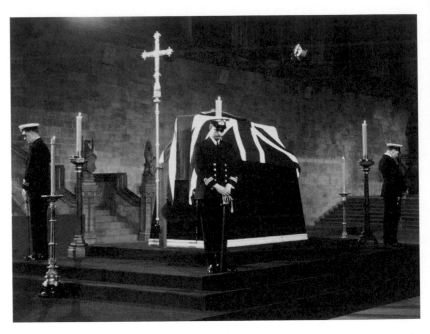

The lying in state of Sir Winston Churchill at Westminster Hall. Royal Navy officers stand guard.
27 January 1965

CHURCHILL IN QUOTES

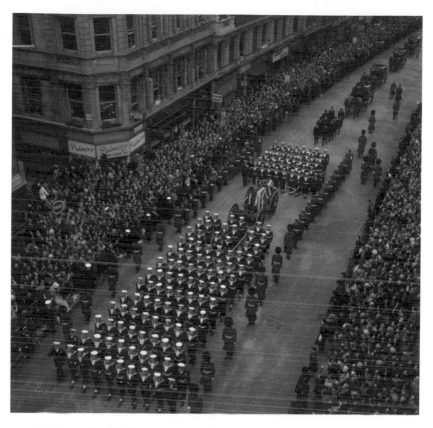

Sir Winston Churchill's funeral cortege makes its way along the Strand on its way from
Westminster to St Paul's Cathedral.
30 January 1965

"Every morn brought forth a noble chance, and every chance brought forth a noble knight."

Speech praising the men of the Royal Air Force for their efforts during the evacuation
of the British Expeditionary Force from Dunkirk, paraphrasing Tennyson in *Morte
d'Arthur*, House of Commons, 4 June 1940.

"I am ready to meet my Maker. Whether my Maker is prepared for the great ordeal of meeting me is another matter."

On his seventy-fifth birthday, in answer to whether he was afraid of death, 1949.

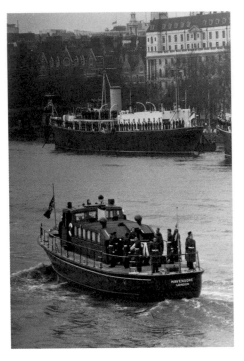

The Port of London Authority launch *Havengore* carries the body of Sir Winston Churchill along the Thames to Waterloo. From there, it would travel by train to Bladon, Oxfordshire.
30 January 1965

"If you are going through hell, keep going."

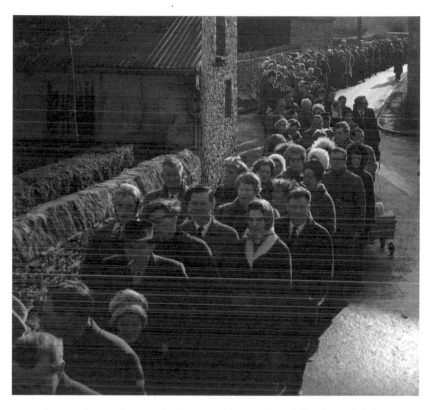

A queue, three or four deep in places, winds its way through the village of Bladon, Oxfordshire, where thousands had arrived by car to file silently past the grave of Sir Winston Churchill in the churchyard.
31 January 1965

"If you go on with this nuclear arms race, all you are going to do is make the rubble bounce."

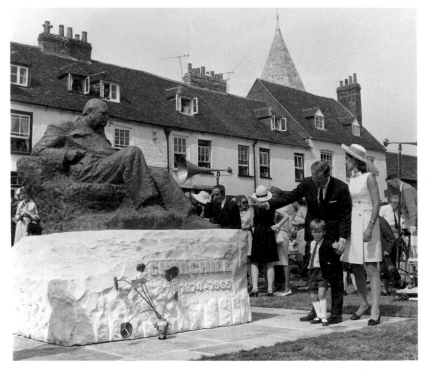

Sir Winston Churchill's grandson, Winston, his wife Minnie and their son Randolph study a sculpture of Sir Winston by Oscar Nemon, which had just been unveiled by Sir Robert Menzies in Westerham, Kent, not far from the great politician's country home, Chartwell.
23 July 1969

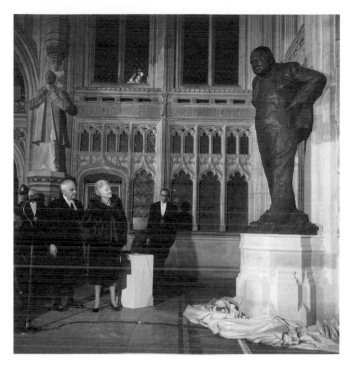

Lady Churchill and Dr Horace King, Speaker of the House of Commons, admire a statue of Sir Winston Churchill that she had just unveiled in the Members' Lobby of the House. The bronze was the work of Oscar Nemon.
1 December 1969

"Baldwin thought Europe was a bore, and Chamberlain thought it was only a greater Birmingham."

"Makes you proud to be British doesn't it?"

Upon being told that a backbench MP had been caught performing indecent acts with a guardsman in St James's Park during one of the coldest February nights in thirty years.

"We are happier in many ways when we are old than when we were young. The young sow wild oats. The old grow sage."

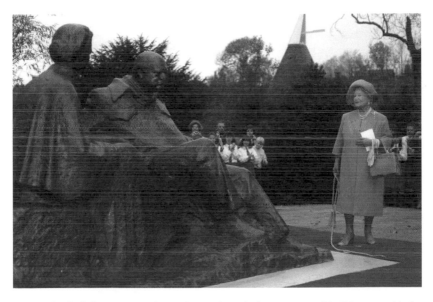

Queen Elizabeth the Queen Mother at the unveiling of a bronze statue of Sir Winston and Lady Churchill at their former country residence, Chartwell, near Westerham, Kent.
13 November 1990

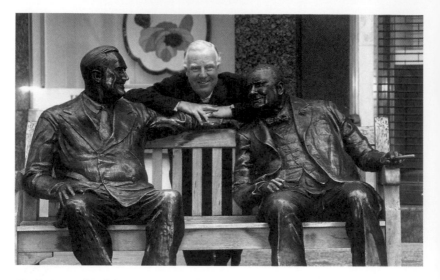

The chairman of English Heritage, Sir Jocelyn Stevens, with a sculpture by Lawrence Holofcener titled *Allies*, which depicts Franklin D. Roosevelt (L) and Winston Churchill in conversation on a bench in New Bond Street, London.
14 March 2000

"One day President Roosevelt told me that he was asking publicly for suggestions about what the war should be called. I said at once 'The Unnecessary War'."

The Second World War, Volume I: The Gathering Storm, 1948.

"My rule of life prescribed as an absolutely sacred rite smoking cigars and also the drinking of alcohol before, after and if need be during all meals and in the intervals between them."

WINSTON LEONARD SPENCER CHURCHILL

1874 Born 30 November to Lord Randolph Churchill, youngest son of John 7th Duke of Marlborough, and American Jennie Jerome at Blenheim Palace, Oxfordshire.

1882–93 Attended St George's School, Ascot, followed by Brunswick School, Hove, and then Harrow School. While at Harrow, joined the Harrow Rifle Corps and became the school fencing champion. Academically, excelled in English and History.

1893–94 Attended Royal Military Academy, Sandhurst, graduating eighth out of 140 in December, 1894. Chose cavalry rather than infantry, as former did not require him to study mathematics, which he hated.

1895 Commissioned as second lieutenant in 4th Queen's Own Hussars (made honorary colonel of regiment in 1941).

1895 Took leave and joined the Spanish Army as an observer during its attempt to quell an insurrection in Cuba. Wrote of his experiences in *The Daily Graphic.*

1896 Posted to India with his regiment; stationed at Bangalore.

1897 In action with Malakand Field Force on Northwest Frontier; mentioned in despatches. Wrote a book detailing his experiences: *The Story of the Malakand Field Force.*

1898 Seconded to 21st Lancers in Sudan; saw action in Battle of Omdurman. Wrote of his experiences in *The River War.*

1899–1900 Left Army; stood as prospective Conservative MP for Oldham, but lost election; travelled to South Africa as war correspondent for *The Morning Post* to cover the Second Anglo-Boer War. Within weeks of arrival, captured by Boers following the ambush of a British armoured reconnaissance train,

during which he rallied the defencers, allowing part of the train to escape. Imprisoned at Pretoria for a month, then escaped, making his way to Durban and becoming a national hero in the process. Joined South African Light Horse cavalry unit, taking part in a number of actions, including Spion Kop, and the Reliefs of Ladysmith and Pretoria.

1900 Returned to UK and elected as Conservative MP for Oldham at the age of 25 years, 10 months, realizing his long-held ambition of becoming a member of Parliament.

1904 Quit Conservative Party over its policy of introducing protective trade tariffs; joined Liberals.

1906 Elected as Liberal MP for North West Manchester. Held many important ministerial posts over the following years. As Home Secretary, joined with Lloyd George to create the Welfare State, and as First Lord of the Admiralty was instrumental in modernizing the Royal Navy.

1915 Resigned from Cabinet following failure of Gallipoli Campaign (the joint British/French invasion of the Dardanelles Peninsula to capture the Ottoman capital of Constantinople during the First World War); rejoined Army in France as commander of an infantry battalion.

1917 Returned to government (now a coalition under Lloyd George) as Minister of Munitions; subsequently became Secretary for War and Secretary for Air (at the same time), followed by Colonial Secretary.

1922 Out of office following collapse of Liberal Party and Lloyd George's coalition government.

1924 Returned to Parliament as an Independent; subsequently rejoined Conservatives to become Chancellor of the Exchequer in Stanley Baldwin's government.

1929–39 Remained an MP, but kept out of office by a succession of prime ministers following his campaign against granting self-government to parts of India, and criticism of Britain's failure to re-arm following the rise of German aggression led by Adolf Hitler.

1939 Invited to rejoin the Conservative government as First Lord of the Admiralty by Neville Chamberlain.

1940 Replaced Neville Chamberlain as Prime Minister at the head of an all-party government. Led the country through the dark days of the Second World War.

1945–51 Out of power after Labour Party's landslide victory in 1945 General Election, but remained leader of the Conservative Party.

1951 Prime Minister again after Conservative success in General Election.

1953 Awarded Nobel Prize in Literature for his many published works, but particularly the six-volume *The Second World War.*

1955 Resigned as Prime Minister at age of 80.

1963 Awarded honorary US citizenship by President John F. Kennedy.

1964 Stood down from Parliament at General Election.

1965 Died on 24 January at the age of 90, lying in State at Palace of Westminster before a funeral held in St Paul's Cathedral. Buried in family plot at St Martin's Church, Bladon, Oxfordshire, near his birthplace and ancestral home, Blenheim Palace.

DECORATIONS

UNITED KINGDOM

Knight Companion, Most Noble Order of the Garter, 1953

Order of Merit, 1946

Order of the Companions of Honour, 1922

India Medal, 1895 (clasp: Punjab Frontier, 1897–98), 1898

Queen's Sudan Medal, 1896–98, 1898

Queen's South Africa Medal, 1899–1902 (clasps: Diamond Hill, Johannesburg, Relief of Ladysmith, Orange Free State, Tugela Heights, Cape Colony), 1901

1914–15 Star, 1919

British War Medal, 1914–18, 1919

Victory Medal, 1920

1939–45 Star, 1945

Africa Star, 1945

Italy Star, 1945

France and Germany Star, 1945

Defence Medal, 1939–45, 1945

War Medal, 1939–45, 1946

King George V Coronation Medal, 1911

King George V Silver Jubilee Medal, 1935

King George VI Coronation Medal, 1937

Queen Elizabeth II Coronation Medal, 1953

Territorial Decoration (King George V), 1924

OTHER NATIONS

Cross of the Order of Military Merit, Spain, 1895

Grand Cordon of the Order of Leopold with Palm, Belgium, 1945

Knight Grand Cross, Order of the Lion of the Netherlands, Holland, 1946

Grand Cross, Order of the Oaken Crown, Luxembourg, 1946

Grand Cross with Chain, Royal Norwegian Order of St Olav, Norway, 1948

Order of the Elephant, Denmark, 1950

Order of Liberation, France, 1958

Most Refulgent Order of the Star of Nepal, Nepal, 1961

Grand Sash of the High Order of Sayhyid Mohammed bin Ali el Senoussi, Libya, 1962

Army Distinguished Service Medal, USA, 1919

War Cross with Palm, Belgium, 1945

Military Medal, 1940–45, Luxembourg, 1946

Military Medal, France, 1947

War Cross with Palm, France, 1947

Cuban Campaign Medal, 1895–98, Spain, 1914

Khedive's Sudan Medal, Egypt, 1899 (clasp: Khartoum)

King Christian X's Liberty Medal, Denmark, 1946

This edition first published 2023 by
Ammonite Press
an imprint of Guild of Master Craftsman Publications Ltd
Castle Place, 166 High Street, Lewes, East Sussex BN7 1XU, United Kingdom

This title has been created with materials first published in Churchill in "Quotes" (2011)
Reprinted 2012 (twice), 2013, 2014, 2015, 2016, 2017, 2018, 2021

Images © Press Association Images
Copyright in the Work © GMC Publications Ltd, 2023

ISBN 978-1-78145-480-0
(ISBN 978-1-90667-261-4 first edition)
All rights reserved

A catalogue record for this book is available from the British Library.

Publisher: Jonathan Bailey
Production: Jim Bulley
Senior Editor: Sara Harper
Design: Robin Shields

Colour reproduction by GMC Reprographics
Printed and bound in China

**AMMONITE
PRESS**   **pa** media

The Publishers gratefully acknowledge Press Association Images,
from whose extensive archives the photographs in this book have been selected.
Copies of the photographs in this book, and many others, may be ordered online
at www.alamy.com